GOD SO LOVED THE WORLD

Traditional Baptists and Calvinism

Fisher Humphreys and Paul E. Robertson

Insight Press
New Orleans, Louisiana

Published by Insight Press, P. O. Box 8369, New Orleans, Louisiana 70182.

Printed in the United States of America.

Library of Congress Cataloging-in-Publication Data

Humphreys, Fisher.
    God so loved the world : traditional Baptists and Calvinism / Fisher Humphreys and Paul E. Robertson.
      p. cm.
    ISBN 0-914520-42-3
    1. Baptists–Doctrines. 2. Calvinism.   I. Robertson, Paul E., 1949- II. Title.
    BX6331.2 .H85 2000
    230'.6–dc21
                  00-010900

To Caroline and Judy

CONTENTS

Preface

We want to thank those who have read and commented on early versions of this book. It is a much better book because of their work than it otherwise would have been. Any errors or infelicities are, of course, our responsibility.

Baptist historian Claude Howe gave us wise guidance with the sections on Baptist history. Members of the Trinity Group—Paul Basden, Gary Furr, Dwight Moody, and Philip Wise—provided important suggestions for all chapters of the book; we regret that the other member of the group, LaMon Brown, was unable to read the book; he was involved in preparing to return to the mission field. Bill Warren also offered helpful insights.

1

Our Purpose

A Tragic Story

The impulse to write this book came in the late 1990s when one of us (Fisher) received an unusual long distance telephone call. The caller was a stranger who said that he preferred not to identify himself or his hometown or his church. This is the story he told.

"I have been a member of a Baptist church in my hometown since I was born," he said. "I grew up in this church, and I was married here. I had hoped to remain here all my life.

"But now I have a problem. A number of months ago our church called a new pastor. I was on the pastor search committee, and I was enthusiastic about the young man we called. But after he had been here for a while I noticed that his preaching seemed different from what we were accustomed to. Sometimes he seemed to be saying that God doesn't love everyone in the world, only Christians.

"Several of us asked him about this, and he agreed to meet with us and discuss it. During the meeting he told us that he is committed to Calvinism. We talked about many things during the meeting. My concern was with whether he believes that God loves all people. He said that he believes that God does not love all people, only Christians, or, as he put it, 'the elect.'

"Dr. Humphreys," the caller said, "I am very upset about this. I have never heard anything like this in my life. What is Calvinism? What does the Bible say about it? Are Baptists supposed to be Calvinists? If so, nobody ever told me anything about it."

Then he added with deep sadness, "I have decided that my family and I must leave our church. I hate to do this more than I can tell you, but I don't feel that I have a choice; I don't want my children to grow up hearing sermons that say that God does not love all the people in the world."

The purpose for which we have written this book is to help traditional Baptists such as this anonymous caller to understand Calvinism and to relate in a Christian way to Calvinists. This purpose has three components: our readers, our subject, and our hope.

Our Readers

First, this book is for traditional Baptists. We are assuming that traditional Baptists are not Calvinists. We think this assumption is warranted for two reasons, one historical and the other demographic.

Historically, the first Baptists were not Calvinists. In chapter 3 we will show that it was at least a quarter of a century after the formation of the first Baptist church before Calvinism entered Baptist churches.

Demographically most Baptists today are not Calvinists. We realize, of course, that many Baptists are committed to Calvinism; in North America the largest group of Baptist churches with this commitment are the Primitive Baptists with more than a million members. We also realize that some individual Baptists are committed to Calvinism even though they are in denominations that are not Calvinistic; that is the case with the pastor in the story above. Nevertheless, the largest Baptist denominations in North America—the Southern Baptist Convention, the National Baptist Convention/USA, the National Baptist Convention of America, the National Missionary Baptist Convention of America, the Progressive National Baptist Convention, and the American Baptist Churches/USA, with a combined total of more than 33 million members—are not committed to Calvinism. Calvinism is a minority view among Baptists in North America. During the past half century millions of Baptists in North America have had little or no contact with Calvinism; thus they are often surprised and sometimes upset when they hear the message of Calvinism.

Calvinists are aware that they are a minority among Baptists generally and among Southern Baptists in particular. One of their scholars has written:

Any casual observer of the contemporary Southern Baptist scene can readily observe that the Doctrines of Grace no longer hold sway over the majority of

Southern Baptist people, or even a significantly large minority of them.[1]

For these historical and demographic reasons we say that traditional Baptists are not Calvinists. Our book is addressed to traditional Baptists.

We have not written the book for Calvinists. If we had intended to engage Calvinists in debate our book would have taken a different form than it presently has; for example, it would be much longer because we would need to review many arguments used by Calvinists and offer detailed responses to them. Our purpose is to help traditional Baptists understand Calvinism, not to debate Calvinists about Calvinism. In other words, this is not a book of polemics; it is a book of theology written out of pastoral concerns.

We have not written our book for non-Christians either. Our book is about an intra-Christian conversation, and, to speak candidly, we do not think that it is an especially edifying conversation for people who are not Christians.

Finally, we have not written our book for Christians in other denominations. Our explanation of Calvinism and our description of an alternative to Calvinism might be useful to persons who are not Baptists, and it would please us if this were the case, but Christians from other denominations will not find in this book an account of the relationship of their

---

[1] Thomas J. Nettles, *By His Grace and For His Glory: A Historical, Theological, and Practical Study of the Doctrines of Grace in Baptist Life* (Grand Rapids: Baker Book House, 1986), 244.

denomination to Calvinism. In this sense our book is primarily for traditional Baptists.

We hope that our book will be useful for all kinds of Baptists. Both of us are members of churches affiliated with the Southern Baptist Convention. The SBC is now at a period in its life in which the claims of Calvinism are being reasserted; the anonymous caller whose story we told above, for example, is a member of a church affiliated with the SBC. Naturally, as we have written our book we have been aware of the fact that Southern Baptists may have a special interest in the subject we address in this book.

Our Subject

Our subject is Calvinism, and we will devote three chapters of the book to explaining Calvinism. For now we will say that Calvinism is the vision of the Christian faith that was taught by the sixteenth-century reformer John Calvin.

Occasionally Calvinism is known by other names. Among Roman Catholics it is sometimes called "Augustinianism." Sometimes Calvinists refer to their theology as "reformed theology" or as "the doctrines of grace."

Our Hope

Our hope is that traditional Baptist readers will come to understand Calvinism so that they will be able to relate to it in a Christian way.

We are convinced that the Christian way of relating to anything must involve both truth and love; we hope that our book will be an example of *speaking the truth in love.*[2]

Both the truth and the love are important to us. We will do our best to be truthful in what we say about Calvinism. We are aware that, because we are traditional Baptists who are not convinced by the claims of Calvinism, we will be tempted to present an unfair caricature of Calvinism. We will certainly try to resist that temptation. We hope that a Calvinist who happens to read our book will be able to say, "You have been fair to Calvinism."

Concerning love, we are fortunate because for many years both of us have had friends who are Calvinists. They are friends whom we like, respect, and appreciate. We have engaged in more conversations with them than we can count. We have learned from them, and we treasure our relationships with them. It would be wrong of us to speak unlovingly of Calvinists.

Some of our readers may not have had friends who are Calvinists, and some such as the anonymous caller whose story we told above have had unpleasant experiences with Calvinism. We understand this, and we realize that it may be difficult for them to feel kindly toward Calvinism. We will be very pleased if our book helps them to relate in a loving way to Calvinists.

---

[2]Eph. 4:15.

2

Understanding Calvinism

Since Calvinism is the vision of the Christian faith that was taught by the sixteenth-century reformer John Calvin, we will begin our study of Calvinism by reviewing his life and work.

John Calvin

John Calvin was one of the greatest leaders that the Christian church has ever had. He was born in France in 1509 and studied to be a lawyer. At about the age of twenty he learned about the Protestant reformation that had been begun a decade earlier by the German monk Martin Luther, and Calvin became a convinced Protestant. Eventually he became the leader of the Protestant church in Geneva, Switzerland. He was a prolific author and an influential preacher and teacher. His *Institutes of the Christian Religion* was initially a brief commentary on the Apostles' Creed, but Calvin repeatedly revised and enlarged it; the final edition, of 1559, is very large and is one of the masterpieces of Christian theology.

Traditional Baptists agree with many of the ideas that Calvin expressed in the *Institutes*. For example, we agree with Calvin that there is one God; that God is the Creator of all things; that God is in some mysterious way Father, Son, and Holy Spirit; that Jesus is the Son of God who suffered and died and rose again to save sinners; and that the church is the people of God.

However, traditional Baptists disagree with some of the other ideas that Calvin expressed in the *Institutes*. For example, traditional Baptists believe in congregational church government. Calvin did not; he believed that congregations should be governed by elders, as is done in Presbyterian churches today. Again, traditional Baptists believe in the separation of church and state as the best way to provide full religious liberty to all citizens. Calvin did not believe in the separation of church and state; he believed that in Christian places such as Geneva the government should give its full support to the church.

So traditional Baptists agree with Calvin about most things but disagree with him about a few things.

But when we talk about Calvinism today we usually are not talking about any of the ideas mentioned above. Instead we are talking about Calvin's doctrine of salvation.

In order to understand Calvin's doctrine of salvation we must bear in mind that Calvin was always concerned to emphasize that God is the sovereign Lord over all things. Traditional Baptists also believe that God is sovereign, but Calvin had a special understanding of God's sovereignty. He understood God's sovereignty to mean that everything that happens is God's will; another way to express this is to say that Calvin believed that God foreordains everything that happens in the world. Calvin wrote, "God does not permit, but governs by his power."[3] As we will see, traditional Baptists do not believe that God foreordains everything that happens; they believe that God foreordains some things and permits others, notably, sin.

Calvin also taught that God foreordains who will be saved and who will not. In other words, God sovereignly decides in advance the final destiny of every human being. This is called *predestination*, and Calvin defined it as follows:

> We call predestination God's eternal decree, by which he compacted with himself what he willed to become of each man. For all are not created in equal condition; rather, eternal life is foreordained for some, eternal damnation for others.[4]

He added: "God by his secret plan freely chooses whom he pleases, rejecting others."[5]

Calvin insisted that God's work of predestination does not depend upon God's foreknowledge of how each person will respond to the gospel. Calvin objected to "covering election

---

[3]All references are to John Calvin, *Institutes of the Christian Religion,* edited by John T. McNeill, translated and indexed by Ford Lewis Battles (Philadelphia: The Westminster Press, 1960). This quotation is found in 3.23.1.

[4]Ibid., 3.21.5.

[5]Ibid., 3.21.7.

with a veil of foreknowledge."[6] He wrote: "God could foresee nothing good in man except what he had already determined to bestow by the benefit of his election."[7] First God predestined; then God foreknew. Traditional Baptists think that the truth is the other way around: first God foreknew who would accept and who would reject the gospel, and then God predestined that the former would be saved and the latter lost.

Calvin was aware that many people have serious problems with his view. Speaking of God's sovereign decision to damn some people Calvin wrote: "The decree is dreadful indeed, I confess."[8] It is dreadful, but it is not unjust, for whatever God does is just: "Whatever he wills, by the very fact that he wills it, must be considered righteous."[9]

Calvin held these views because he believed that they were taught in the Bible; in chapter 5 we will discuss some of the biblical passages to which Calvin appealed.

Calvin also thought that his view was consistent. For example, he insisted that, even though from eternity God has willed everything that happens in this world, including sin, nevertheless God is not the author of sin: "Man falls [into sin] according as God's providence ordains, but he falls by his own fault."[10] Traditional Baptists do not believe that "God's providence ordains" that human beings sin, and they find it

---

[6]Ibid., 3.22.1.

[7]Ibid., 3.22.5.

[8]Ibid., 3.23.7.

[9]Ibid., 3.23.2.

[10]Ibid., 3.23.8.

difficult to understand how one can say that God foreordained that human beings would sin without suggesting that in some sense God is the author of sin.

Calvin also taught that it is appropriate to proclaim the gospel to all people even though God has predestined that some of them will be damned. God "ordained from eternity those whom he wills to embrace in love, and those upon whom he wills to vent his wrath. Yet he announces salvation to all men indiscriminately."[11]

Calvin was not the first Christian theologian to emphasize predestination. The church father Augustine, who died in A.D. 430, stressed predestination; so did the greatest of the medieval theologians, Thomas Aquinas, and the first of the great Protestant reformers, Martin Luther. Calvin drew upon the work of his predecessors, but his own contribution to this subject is so great that it is appropriate that we today refer to this understanding of predestination as "Calvinism." One of his biographers said that Calvin "was the most lucid writer in Europe" in the sixteenth century.[12] Using language that was clear and forceful, drawing upon a wide array of biblical texts, making judicious use of the work of his predecessors, Calvin presented a Protestant version of God's sovereign work of predestination that has continued to engage the minds of Christians ever since.

---

[11] Ibid., 3.24.17.

[12] T. H. L. Parker, *John Calvin* (London: J. M. Dent & Son Ltd, 1975), 98.

The Synod of Dort

Calvin's vision of the Christian faith was widely disseminated in the sixteenth century, and it became the dominant vision of Christianity in places as diverse as Switzerland, the Netherlands, and Scotland. It was embraced by Puritans both inside and outside the Church of England, and they brought it to the American colonies.

An excellent presentation of Calvinism was developed in the Netherlands in the seventeenth century. The story of how this occurred is a fascinating one, and we will review it because of its enormous influence on Calvinism in North America today.

Apparently the first Protestants in the Netherlands were not Calvinists.[13] In the sixteenth century the Netherlands provided considerable religious freedom, as a result of which numerous Calvinists who were not welcome in their homelands emigrated to the Netherlands; over time the Protestant church in the Netherlands became Calvinistic.

Late in the sixteenth century a theologian of the church, Jacobus Arminius, began to criticize the Calvinistic doctrine

---

[13]We have drawn principally upon three sources for the history of Arminius and the Synod of Dort. They are Carl Bangs, *Arminius: A Study in the Dutch Reformation* (Nashville: Abingdon Press, 1971); Jack Rogers, "The Synod of Dort and the Arminian Controversy (A.D. 1619)," *Case Studies in Christ and Salvation*, by Jack Rogers, Ross Mackenzie, and Louis Weeks (Philadelphia: The Westminster Press, 1977); and Philip Schaff, editor, *The Creeds of Christendom: With a History and Critical Notes*, sixth edition (Grand Rapids: Baker Book House, 1993).

of predestination. He did not believe that God created some persons to be saved and others to be damned. Instead he understood the biblical teaching about predestination to be that God decreed that those persons who accepted Christ would be saved and those who rejected Christ would be lost. This is, of course, the view that is accepted by traditional Baptists today.

Arminius's contribution to a non-Calvinistic understanding of predestination and related matters is so great that it is now customary to refer to Protestants who disagree with Calvinism as "Arminians." However, as we will show below, traditional Baptists do not accept some of the other things that Arminius taught, and for that reason in this book we are not using the word "Arminian" to describe traditional Baptist theology.

Arminius's views became the occasion for prolonged conflict in the Netherlands, but the conflict was not settled during Arminius's lifetime. In 1610, the year after Arminius died, his followers in the Netherlands published a document called a remonstrance, that is, a protest. For this reason it is customary to call the followers of Arminius the Remonstrants. Their document contained five articles.

The first article is about predestination. The Remonstrants did not directly deny the Calvinistic doctrine that God sovereignly predestined some individuals to be saved and others to be damned. What they did was rather to replace the Calvinistic understanding of predestination with Arminius's idea that God predestined that those people who accepted

Christ would be saved and that those who rejected Christ would be lost.[14]

The second article of the Remonstrants is about Christ's death. The Remonstrants affirmed that "Jesus Christ, the Saviour of the world, died for all men and for every man."

The third article is about the effects of sin upon people's lives. In it the Remonstrants said that it is impossible for people to do anything that pleases God unless God helps them in advance.

The fourth article is about God's grace. In it the Remonstrants said that God offers grace freely but that human beings can, if they so choose, reject God's offer of grace.

The fifth and final article is about whether Christians can lose their salvation. The Remonstrants did not take a position on this issue; instead they wrote that they needed to study the Scriptures more carefully in order to learn the truth about this difficult question.

These five articles of the Remonstrants are similar to what traditional Baptists believe, but they are not identical. Traditional Baptists agree with the Remonstrants that God predestines to save those who believe in Christ and to leave in their sins those who reject Christ. We also agree that Christ died for all people. We agree that people must have God's help in order to respond to the gospel with faith; however, unlike the Remonstrants, traditional Baptists believe that God has already given that help to all people by creating them with the capacity for faith. Traditional Baptists agree with the

---

[14]This and the following references to the Arminian Articles are to Philip Schaff, ed., *The Creeds of Christendom*, III:545-49.

Remonstrants that God offers grace freely to all people but that people can, and unfortunately sometimes do, reject God's offer of grace. Finally, whereas the Remonstrants were uncertain about whether true Christians can ever lose their salvation, traditional Baptists believe that God will always preserve believers so that, even though they fall into sin, in the end they will be saved.

Shortly before his death in 1609 Arminius had called for the church in the Netherlands to convene an official council to discuss these contested ideas. After his death the church, supported by the government, convened the council. It was held in 1618-19 in the city of Dort, and it was called the Synod of Dort; today the city of Dort is called "Dordrecht."

At the Synod the church leaders discussed the theology of Arminius in general and the five articles of his followers the Remonstrants in particular. But the Synod did not provide an open forum for the discussion of the contested issues; instead it was controlled by the Calvinists, and the Remonstrants were called in only to hear charges brought against them. After the Synod had completed its work the government expelled two hundred clergy from the ministry and sent eighty of them into exile. Then, on May 14, 1619, the government beheaded one of the leaders of the Remonstrants, John Oldenbarneveldt, an event that serves as a vivid reminder of the fact that in the Netherlands in the seventeenth century the church and the state were not separate.

This brings us to our primary concern in this section, which is the document issued by the Calvinists at the Synod of Dort. It is known as the *Canons of Dort*, and it is organized under five heads of doctrine, each of which is a reply to one of the five articles of the Remonstrants.

Today many Calvinists in North America summarize their theology in terms of the five points made by the Calvinists at Dort. One of the reasons they do this is that in English it is possible to make an acronym for the five points of Dort using the word *TULIP*, and, of course, the Netherlands are famous for their tulips. The acronym is as follows: *T*otal depravity, *U*nconditional election, *L*imited atonement, *I*rresistible grace, and the *P*erseverance of believers.

This is a useful device, but we immediately notice several things about it. First, we today use the word *predestination* more than the word *election*, so for us it is clearer to call the second point *unconditional predestination*. Second, the sequence of the five points is not the sequence of the points made by the Remonstrants. Third, the sequence for the five points is not logical. Logically predestination should be the first point; it is the principal point, and the sense of the other points is affected by what is said about predestination.

In fact, predestination did come first in the *Canons*; and it was followed by limited atonement. In other words, at Dort the sequence was *ULTIP* rather than *TULIP*. We will review the five points of Dort in the order in which they appear in the *Canons*, which is also the logical order.

First, unconditional predestination. Predestination is in two parts; the predestination of certain people to be saved is called *election*, and the predestination of other people to be lost is called *reprobation*. Here is part of what the Calvinists at Dort wrote about election:

Election is the unchangeable purpose of God, whereby, before the foundation of the world, he hath, out of mere grace, according to the sovereign good pleasure of his own will, chosen, from the whole human race, which had fallen through their own fault . . . a certain number of persons to redemption in Christ. . . . This election was not founded upon foreseen faith.[15]

As we saw above this was also the view of Calvin. The Calvinists at Dort wrote the following concerning the other side of predestination, namely, the predestination of some to be damned:

What peculiarly tends to illustrate and recommend to us the eternal and unmerited grace of election is the express testimony of sacred Scripture, that not all, but some only, are elected, while others are passed by in the eternal decree; whom God, out of his sovereign, most just, irreprehensible and unchangeable good pleasure, hath decreed to leave in the common misery into which they have willfully plunged themselves, and not to bestow upon them saving faith and the grace of conversion. . . . And this is the decree of reprobation.

These ideas are very different from traditional Baptist theology. Traditional Baptists do not believe that God chose

---

[15]This and the following references to the *Canons of Dort* are to Philip Schaff, editor, *The Creeds of Christendom*, III:581-97.

some to be saved and passed by others whom God might have saved; instead we believe that God reaches out in love to all people. Traditional Baptists believe that the reason that people are lost is not that God passes by them but that they reject God's offer of salvation.

The second article in the *Canons* is about Christ's limited atonement. Interestingly this article is frequently misunderstood by Calvinists and non-Calvinists alike. The Synod spoke of Christ's death as a satisfaction for sins. They said that the satisfaction that Christ offered "is of infinite worth and value, abundantly sufficient to expiate the sins of the whole world." In other words, the value of the sacrifice that Christ offered was unlimited. What then was limited about limited atonement? The answer is that the purpose of God was limited. It was God's purpose that only the elect, not the reprobate, would benefit from the sacrifice that Christ provided. This follows naturally from the article on predestination.

This idea is also very different from traditional Baptist theology. Traditional Baptists believe that God's purpose was that Christ's death would provide salvation for all the people in the world.

Third, the effects of sin. The Synod said that people are dead in their sins; therefore they are not able, when they hear the gospel, to repent and put their faith in Christ. In order to be able to repent and believe, they must first be born again. God sovereignly causes the elect to be born again, and then they are able to repent and have faith.

Traditional Baptists do not agree. They think that spiritual deadness means that human beings cannot save themselves, but they do not think that it means that human beings cannot repent and have faith in Christ. Traditional Baptists believe that the new birth happens after people repent and have faith in Christ, not before.

Fourth, God's grace. The Synod said that God's grace that leads to the new birth is irresistible. It is carried out by God in mysterious ways deep within the inmost recesses of the hearts of the elect—and only the elect—so that they will respond to the gospel with repentance and faith.

Traditional Baptists do not agree. They think that God offers grace freely to all human beings and that some accept it. Others, however, resist and finally reject God's offer of grace. Grace is not irresistible; it is resistible, and, sadly, some people resist it.

Fifth and finally, the Synod of Dort said God sovereignly preserves the elect so that they can never fall away from the faith. They are tempted and they often yield to temptation, but in the end they are preserved by God from losing their salvation. On this point most traditional Baptists agree with the Synod of Dort rather than with the Remonstrants.

These are the five points of Calvinism, and their influence upon Calvinism today is immense.

We believe that the issue of predestination dominates the other issues. As complex as the issues of sin, atonement, and grace are, how we deal with them is dependent upon how we answer one simple question: Did the sovereign God decide in advance to save certain individuals and to damn others? Calvinists answer Yes; traditional Baptists answer No.

Millard Erickson

In order to bring our presentation of Calvinism into our own time we will summarize the views of a contemporary theologian who is a Calvinist. We have chosen for this purpose Dr. Millard Erickson, who is on the faculty of the Truett Seminary of Baylor University in Waco, Texas.

We have chosen Dr. Erickson's work for several reasons. We are writing principally for Baptists, and Dr. Erickson is a Baptist. In his presentation of Calvinism he has been sensitive to the concerns of traditional Baptists. Dr. Erickson is immensely learned about the literature of Calvinism, and he is very wise about the theology of Calvinism. He is a prolific author. His *Christian Theology* is one of the most widely used theology textbooks in North America. Perhaps most important of all, he has a beautiful, kind spirit.

We will summarize his views as they appear in his *Systematic Theology*,[16] a book that is 1300 pages long and has 60 chapters, two of which are of special interest to us here. Chapter 17, entitled "God's Plan," is about what Calvinists have traditionally called the decrees of God. Erickson uses the word *plan* rather than the conventional word *decrees* to refer to everything that from eternity God has foreordained or predestined or willed or decided will happen in the world. Erickson says that God's plan is not so much an imperative as it is a description of what will happen:

---

[16]Millard Erickson, *Systematic Theology*, second edition (Grand Rapids: Baker Book House, 1998).

To be sure, what God has decided will come to pass does involve an element of necessity. The particulars of God's plan, however, should be thought of less as imperatives than as descriptions of what will occur. The plan of God does not force human to act in particular ways, but renders it certain that they will *freely* act in those ways.[17]

Erickson says that God's plan has priority over human freedom:

With respect to the particular matter of the acceptance or rejection of salvation, God in his plan has chosen that some shall believe and thus receive the offer of salvation. He foreknows what will happen because he has decided what is to happen. This is true with respect to all other human decisions and actions as well. God is not dependent upon what humans decide. . . . God's decision has rendered it certain that every individual will act in a particular way.[18]

If God's decision renders it certain that human beings will act in particular ways, then are human beings free? Erickson believes that they are, and he argues that God's plan is compatible with real human freedom. He writes:

---

[17]Ibid., 380.

[18]Ibid., 381.

At this point we must raise the question of whether God can create genuinely free beings and yet render certain all things that are to come to pass, including the free decisions and actions of those beings. The key to unlocking the problem is the distinction between rendering something certain and rendering it necessary. The former is a matter of God's decision that something *will* happen; the latter is a matter of his decreeing that it *must* occur. In the former case, the human being will not act in a way contrary to the course of action God has chosen; in the latter case, the human being cannot act in a way contrary to what God has chosen. What we are saying is that God renders it certain that a person who could act (or could have acted) differently does in fact act in a particular way (the way that God wills).[19]

According to Dr. Erickson, freedom means that human beings are not under constraint. They are free to do what pleases them. However, they have no control over what pleases them and what does not; those things are controlled by God's decree. "Who I am is a result of God's decision and activity."[20] This view may be called *congruism* or *compatibilism* because it says that God's sovereign plan is congruent with or compatible with a genuine choice on the part of human beings.

---

[19]Ibid., 383.

[20]Ibid., 384.

In summary, "God has rendered certain everything that occurs,"[21] yet human beings make free decisions.

Here we offer three observations. First, Dr. Erickson places much more emphasis on human freedom than did John Calvin or the Calvinists at the Synod of Dort. Second, interest in human freedom is very high in our world today; it is associated in people's minds with moral seriousness: if you are not free, you cannot be truly good or bad. It also is associated with the dignity of human beings; indeed, it is now customary to express the dignity of human beings in terms of their right to freedom of religion, freedom of speech, freedom of the press, and so on. Therefore it is understandable that Dr. Erickson would be more interested in affirming this important fact about human beings than his theological predecessors in the sixteenth and seventeenth centuries were. Third, we do not know whether compatibilism is a coherent idea or not; certainly it runs counter to the widespread intuition that human decisions cannot be free if God actually decided them in advance. If compatibilism is true, that relieves the tension between Calvinism's understanding of God's sovereignty and human freedom, but it does nothing to relieve the difficulties that are inherent in the doctrine of predestination itself, namely, that a loving God predestined that some persons be damned.

In chapter 44 Erickson deals with predestination in particular. Following an informative summary of the thinking of other people, he offers his own carefully nuanced version of Calvinism. He begins by observing that the Bible teaches

---

[21]Ibid., 387.

that God sovereignly elects certain individuals for salvation. He then says that the Bible also teaches that human beings are spiritually dead and so are unable to respond to the gospel. Therefore,

> Brought back to the question of why some believe, we do find an impressive collection of texts suggesting that God has selected some to be saved, and that our response to the offer of salvation depends upon this prior decision and initiative by God.[22]

Then Erickson considers the claims of non-Calvinists that God has predestined certain individuals to be saved because God has foreknown their response to the gospel. He says that this claim is not supported by Scripture. Foreknowledge is not the grounds for predestination but rather the confirmation of it, he writes.

Next Erickson addresses the offer of salvation to all people. Is it a genuine offer if in fact people are incapable of accepting it because of their spiritual deadness? Yes, he replies, the offer is genuine, even though people are unable to respond without special enablements from God:

> Humans in the unregenerate state are totally depraved and unable to respond to God's grace, [and therefore]

---

[22]Ibid., 938.

there is no question as to whether they are free to accept the offer of salvation—no one is![23]

Conclusion

Dr. Erickson has provided an orderly and sensitive presentation of Calvinism, perhaps as winsome as can be made to contemporary traditional Baptist readers. In Erickson as in Calvin himself and in the *Canons of Dort*, the issue that concerns us most is predestination. In view of that fact, from this point forward in the book we intend routinely to use the word "Calvinism" to refer to the understanding of predestination that we have found in John Calvin, in the Synod of Dort, and in Millard Erickson. We acknowledge that there is much more to Calvinism than its view of predestination, but our concern in this book is for that view in particular.

In spite of all of the thoughtful arguments made by Calvinists past and present, we, along with other traditional Baptists, remain unconvinced that God has done what Calvinists say, namely, decide the final destinies of individuals in advance of their decisions and independently of God's foreknowledge of their decisions.

Here we want to emphasize that we traditional Baptists agree with the Calvinists that God is the sovereign Lord of the universe. This is a very important issue to us. We do not think that what is at stake here is the relationship between the sovereignty of God and the freedom of human beings. In fact,

---

[23]Ibid., 927.

if we ourselves had to choose between God's sovereignty and human freedom, we would choose God's sovereignty, for there is no hope for human beings if God is not the sovereign Lord of the universe.

No, the question is not whether God is sovereign; God is. The question is, How does God exercise sovereignty? What has God sovereignly decided to do in the world?

We believe that God could have decided to do what Calvinists believe God has done, namely, predestine some individuals to salvation and others to damnation. God has the power and the knowledge to do that. But we believe that is not what God decided to do. As traditional Baptists we believe that God sovereignly decided to create human beings with the freedom to decide whether to accept or to reject the offer of the gospel. We believe that God sovereignly decided to respect the decisions that human beings make. We believe that God sovereignly decided (predestined) that those who accept Jesus Christ will be saved and that those who reject Jesus Christ will be lost.

As traditional Baptists we think that the decisions of human beings—to act righteously or to sin, to accept the gospel or to reject it—are just that, decisions of human beings. We do not think that they are the decisions of God. We do not believe that God would ever will that anyone sin or that anyone be damned. God's will is that human beings always act righteously and, once they have sinned, God's will is that they all be saved.

But we are getting ahead of ourselves. Before presenting the theology of traditional Baptists we need to consider the place of Calvinism in Baptist history. We will do that in the next chapter.

3

Calvinism in Baptist History

The First Baptists

The first Baptists were not Calvinists.

The first Baptists were English people who had emigrated to the Netherlands in order to escape persecution for having separated from the established Church of England. After they arrived in the Netherlands they came to the conviction that the New Testament teaches that only believers should be baptized. Sometime during the winter of 1608-1609 their pastor, John Smyth, baptized first himself and then the others, and the first Baptist church came into being.[24]

Because they were living in the Netherlands the first Baptists were aware of the conflict that was going on between Arminius and the Calvinists there. In 1609—the year that Arminius died—John Smyth drew up a confession of his faith. It contains twenty articles, in one of which he expresses the conviction

---

[24]The principal source for most of the history in this chapter is Leon McBeth, *The Baptist Heritage* (Nashville: Broadman Press, 1987).

that men, of the grace of God through the redemption of Christ, are able (the Holy Spirit, by grace, being before unto them *grace prevemènt*) to repent, to believe, to turn to God, and to attain to eternal life; so on the other hand, they are able themselves to resist the Holy Spirit, to depart from God, and to perish forever.[25]

This is a forceful rejection of the Calvinistic claims that people are unable to respond to the gospel and that God's grace is irresistible, and it is the view of traditional Baptists today. God has taken the initiative of giving people prevenient (the word means *coming before*) grace that enables them, even though they are sinners, either to accept or to reject the gospel.

By the following year, 1610—the year of the *Remonstrance*—a few members of the Baptist church had separated from the others and were being led by a layman, Thomas Helwys. Helwys led them to return to London, but before they left they prepared a confession of faith in Latin which includes nineteen articles; it is called "A Short Confession of Faith." In the sixth article they said that the predestination of individuals is a product of God's foreknowledge of how individuals respond. In the seventh article they wrote:

---

[25]"Short Confession of Faith in XX Articles by John Smyth," article 9. This and the other Baptist confessions quoted below are found in William L. Lumpkin, *Baptist Confessions of Faith* (Chicago: The Judson Press, 1959); see 100-01.

For being perfect goodness and love itself (following the nature of love and perfect goodness) [God] willeth the health, good, and happiness of his creatures; therefore hath he predestinated that none of them should be condemned.[26]

Traditional Baptists today hold exactly these views: God has not predestined either that human beings sin or that they be damned, for God's will is that all be saved.

And in the following year, 1611—the year that the King James Version of the Bible was first published—Thomas Helwys published another confession of faith entitled "A Declaration of Faith of English People Remaining at Amsterdam in Holland." It has twenty-seven articles, and it is vigorously anti-Calvinistic. In the original archaic but charming language article 5 reads as follows:

That GOD before the Foundatiō off the World hath Predestinated that all that beleeve in him shall-be saved, Ephes. 1.4, 12; Mark 16.16. and al that beleeve not shallbee damned. Mark 16.16. all which he knewe before. Rom. 8.29. And this is the Election and reprobacion spoken of in the Scripturs, concerning salvacion, and condemnacion, and not that GOD hath Predestinated men to bee wicked, and so to bee damned, but that men being wicked shallbee damned, for GOD would have all men saved, and come to the knowledg off the truth, I Tim. 2.4. and would have no

---

man to perish, but would have all men come to repentance. 2 Pet. 3.9. and willeth not the death of him that deith. Ezec. 18.32. And therefore GOD is the author off no mens comdemnacion, according to the saieing off the Prophet. Osæa. 13. Thy distruction O Israel, is off thy selfe, but thy helpe is off mee.[27]

Here once more we have a ringing affirmation of what we think we are entitled to call the traditional Baptist view: God has not predestined either that human beings sin or that they be damned. God wants all people to be saved. What God has predestined is that those who accept the gospel will be saved and that those who reject it will be lost.

These three confessions were written in the first three years after the formation of the first Baptist church, and in them the earliest Baptists made it clear that they were not Calvinists. How, then, did Calvinism come into Baptist life? When did it happen?

---

[27]Ibid., 118.

The Arrival of Calvinism

In the seventeenth century many of the finest Christians both inside and outside the Church of England were Puritans and Calvinists. A quarter of a century after the formation of the first Baptist church seventeen members of a Separatist Puritan congregation in London became convinced of the appropriateness of believers baptism. On September 12, 1633, they "desired dismission [from their own church in order] that they might become an Entire Church, & further ye Communion of those Churches in Order amongst themselves, wch at last was granted to them."[28] Once they had been dismissed from their own church—no later than 1638—and had been baptized as believers, they effectively became a new Baptist church. Since they were Calvinists, the church that they formed was the first Baptist church with a Calvinistic theology. This church was in London, and its pastor was Samuel Eaton. By 1644 there were seven Calvinistic Baptist churches in and near London, and they issued a confession of faith that we now call *The First London Confession*. It is, of course, a Calvinistic document, and the third article includes the following:

> God had in Christ before the foundation of the world, according to the good pleasure of his will, fore-ordained some men to eternall life through Jesus Christ, to the praise and glory of his grace, leaving the

---

[28]Leon McBeth, *The Baptist Heritage*, 43.

rest in their sinne to their just condemnation, to the praise of his Justice.[29]

It is sometimes said that the early Baptists divided into Calvinistic and non-Calvinistic groups, but this is not accurate. The truth is rather that the two groups of Baptist churches came into being more or less independently of each other. From the beginning the two groups were fully aware of their differences, and they continued to operate separately from each other. The original Baptists and their spiritual descendants came to be known as *General Baptists* because they believed that Christ died to save all people in general; the Calvinistic newcomers came to be known as *Particular Baptists* because they believed that Christ died to save only the elect, not to save all people.

The two groups of churches both grew during the seventeenth century, but the Particular Baptists grew much faster than the General Baptists. One reason for this was that their Calvinism made them attractive to their contemporaries. Among the Puritans who dominated so much of English life in the seventeenth century Calvinism was almost universally accepted, so it was relatively easy to move from Puritanism into a Particular Baptist church. On the other hand it was much more difficult to move from Puritanism into a General Baptist church because that move involved surrendering one's Calvinism.[30]

---

[29]Lumpkin, *Baptist Confessions*, 157.

[30]Barrington E. White, "The English Particular Baptists and the Great Rebellion, 1640-1660," *Baptist History and Heritage* 9:1

In 1689 Parliament passed the Act of Toleration, which meant that Baptist churches were no longer illegal in England. One might assume that this new freedom would have led Baptist church life in England to flourish, but unfortunately that did not happen. What happened instead was that both groups of Baptists developed severe problems. Many of the General Baptists were influenced by the rationalism and skepticism that characterized much of English life in the eighteenth century, and they drifted from orthodox Christianity into deism or Unitarianism. And many of the Particular Baptists moved away from the warmhearted faith characteristic of early Baptist life into a cold and rigid hyper-Calvinism that was militantly opposed to evangelism and missions.

Providentially, a great renewal of Christian faith also occurred in the eighteenth century. It is known by several names: the Wesleyan revival, the evangelical revival, the First Great Awakening, revivalism, or simply the Revival. In America it was led by a Congregationalist pastor in Massachusetts, Jonathan Edwards. Interestingly, in England it was led by two Anglican priests, one an Arminian and the other a Calvinist. The Arminian was John Wesley, the founder of Methodism, and the Calvinist was his younger friend, George Whitefield.

Revivalism brought about renewal in the life not only of the churches in which it had begun, the Anglican and the Congregational, but in other churches as well. Both in England and in America Baptists were profoundly influenced

---

(January 1974), 17.

by revivalism; revivalism helped the Calvinistic Baptists to shake off their hyper-Calvinism and become evangelistic again, and it helped the non-Calvinistic Baptists to shake off their skepticism and rationalism.

One of the most important results of the renewal of Baptist life was the launching of the modern missionary movement. In 1792 William Carey, a Baptist pastor and a cobbler, was sent by the newly organized Baptist Missionary Society as a missionary to India.

Throughout most of the nineteenth century in England the General and Particular Baptists continued to function as separate groups, but in 1891 they were merged into one group, though many Baptist churches were suspicious of the merger and refused to join it.

Now we will look briefly at Baptists and Calvinism in America.

Baptists and Calvinism in America

The first Baptist church in America was established in Providence, Rhode Island, in 1639 by Roger Williams, the founder of the colony of Rhode Island.[31] Williams was born in London. In 1627 he was graduated from Cambridge University and ordained in the Church of England. By 1629 he had become a Separatist Puritan, and in 1631 he and his

---

[31]On Roger Williams see Edwin S. Gaustad, *Liberty of Conscience: Roger Williams in America* (Grand Rapids: Wm. B. Eerdmans Publishing Company, 1991).

wife Mary emigrated to Massachusetts. For two years he served as pastor of the church in Salem, but his commitment to religious liberty resulted in trouble with the authorities in the colony. Early in 1636 the Puritan authorities exiled Williams from Massachusetts, and he went into the wilderness where he was cared for by Indians. He purchased land from the Indians and established Providence Plantation, which we know as Rhode Island; unlike the other colonies Rhode Island was established with a full separation of church and state and with full religious liberty for all citizens. In 1639 Williams founded the Baptist church at Providence. In 1644 he traveled to England to secure a charter for the new colony. He died in 1683.

Williams is best remembered for his radical commitment to the separation of church and state and for his kindness to Indians, whose languages he learned and to whom he preached on hundreds of occasions. He did not remain a Baptist very long, but his founding of a colony with religious liberty and his establishment of the first Baptist church in America are contributions that continue to affect the lives of Americans today.

Williams was a Calvinist, and the Baptist church that he founded was a Particular Baptist church. However, it quickly accepted into its membership persons who were General Baptists. In other words, Calvinists and non-Calvinists came together in the first Baptist church in America. The same was true of the second Baptist church in the colonies, one that was established in Newport, Rhode Island, with John Clarke as its pastor. After a few years, however, that church divided into two groups, one Calvinistic and one not.

In America as in England the Calvinistic Baptists initially grew more rapidly than the non-Calvinistic ones. However, in America, unlike England, the Great Awakening altered that fact dramatically. As the Awakening spread in America during the eighteenth century, Baptists experienced the greatest numerical growth of any group. They began as a tiny sect, but they have grown so dramatically from the eighteenth century until today that they are now the largest Protestant group in North America. Some Baptists resisted revivalism, and consequently they did not experience dramatic numerical growth, but many Baptists embraced revivalism enthusiastically and grew dramatically.

Initially the theology of the revivalistic Baptists was Calvinistic. However, their practice of revivalism gradually affected their theology. We often speak of the fact that our beliefs affect our practices, and that is true. The reverse is also true: our practices affect our beliefs. The practice of revivalism made Calvinistic theology seem less and less plausible, and some Baptists began to tone down their Calvinism. An example of this is "The New Hampshire Confession of Faith" of 1833. It was not an official document among New Hampshire Baptists, but it was widely distributed among Baptists in the south. In it the language of Calvinism and predestination have begun to be muted.

The story of the decline of Calvinistic theology among Southern Baptist academic theologians has been told by Paul Basden.[32] It is difficult to chronicle the decline of Calvinism

---

[32] Paul A. Basden, "Predestination" in *Has Our Theology Changed?* ed. Paul A. Basden (Nashville: Broadman & Holman

among Baptist people, but it is clear that during most of the twentieth century the vast majority of Baptists in North America were not Calvinists. That is one reason that in this book we refer to Baptists who are not Calvinists as traditional Baptists. The majority of Baptists today, like the original Baptists of 1608-1609, are not Calvinists.

Conclusion

We have attempted to trace briefly the history of the relationship between Baptists and Calvinism because one of the things that troubles traditional Baptists who encounter Calvinism is whether they are obligated by their Baptist heritage to become Calvinists. The history that we have summarized makes it clear that the answer to that question is No. Baptists who want to be true to their Baptist heritage have no obligation to become Calvinists. The earliest Baptists were not Calvinists, and neither are the great majority of Baptists today.

Calvinistic Baptist scholars are, of course, aware of these two facts. Nevertheless, they sometimes claim that Calvinism is the primary Baptist tradition. We acknowledge that their claim is warranted in the sense that through most of the first three centuries of Baptist history a majority of the most influential Baptist leaders were Calvinists. Furthermore, we acknowledge that Baptists today are indebted to Calvinistic Baptist leaders such as John Bunyan, Roger Williams, John

---

Publishers, 1994).

Gill, Isaac Backus, Richard Furman, William Carey, James Boyce, and Charles Haddon Spurgeon.

Still, it remains the case that the first Baptists were not Calvinists and that the vast majority of Baptists today are not Calvinists, and for those two reasons we believe it is appropriate, when writing about the doctrine of salvation in general and of predestination in particular, to refer to those who reject Calvinism as traditional Baptists.

There is, of course, another question that concerns many traditional Baptists when they learn about Calvinism, and it is the question of what the Bible says about predestination. To that important question we now turn our attention.

4

Scripture: Common Ground

Both traditional Baptists and Calvinists believe in the authority of the Bible as God's Word, and both accept the Bible as the primary source of our doctrinal understanding.

These are important points because in debates between traditional Baptists and Calvinists one group or the other may be tempted to claim that its view alone is biblical. That is a mistake; the truth is rather than both groups are attempting to understand what the Bible teaches.

Why Traditional Baptists and Calvinists Disagree

Why, then, do they disagree? There are, we think, two reasons. One is that there are many passages that, if we take them at face value, support the traditional Baptist view, but there also are many passages that, if we take them at face value, support Calvinism. Traditional Baptists take their passages at face value and then interpret the Calvinists' passages in a way different from what they appear at face value to say. Calvinists do the same thing; they take their passages at face value and then interpret the traditional Baptists' passages in a way different from what they appear at face value to say. In the next two chapters we will review the two sets of passages.

Another reason that traditional Baptists and Calvinists disagree is that the interpretation of Scripture can be very difficult. The Bible is the most profound book in the world, so it is not surprising that conscientious Christians sometimes interpret passages to have very different meanings.

For this reason it is important to ask for the guidance of the Holy Spirit when we study the Bible. Also, it is best to interpret the Scriptures in fellowship with other Christians; so we invite you to join with us in searching them and seeking the truth that God has communicated in them.

In this chapter we will review some biblical passages that traditional Baptists and Calvinists interpret in the same way. Then in chapter 5 we will examine some Scripture passages that on face value support Calvinism, and in chapter 6 we will examine some Scripture passages that on face value support the traditional Baptist beliefs.

Passages We Have in Common

Traditional Baptists and Calvinists agree in their interpretation of the many passages in which it is asserted that God
is sovereign. Calvinists sometimes assert that they are more
committed to God's sovereignty than traditional Baptists, but
they are not; traditional Baptists believe that God is sovereign
over all creation. We believe that God is "the high and exalted
One Who lives forever, whose name is Holy" (Is. 57:15a). We
share the testimony of Daniel:

> I blessed the Most High and praised and honored Him
> who lives forever; for His dominion is an everlasting
> dominion, and His kingdom *endures* from generation
> to generation. All the inhabitants of the earth are
> accounted as nothing, but He does according to His
> will in the host of heaven And *among* the inhabitants
> of earth; And no one can ward off His hand. Or say to
> Him, "What have You done?"[33]

Paul echoes this in Romans 1:20-21:

> For since the creation of the world His invisible
> attributes, His eternal power and divine nature, have
> been clearly seen, being understood through what has
> been made, so that they are without excuse.[34]

---

[33]Dan. 4:34b-35.

[34]See also Mal. 3:6; Dt. 32:27; Is. 45:1ff.; Rom 9:17ff.; Eph.
1:11.

In Psalms we read:

> By the word of the LORD the heavens were made, and
> by the breath of His mouth all their host. He gathers
> the waters of the sea together as a heap; He lays up the
> deeps in storehouses. Let all the earth fear the LORD;
> let all the inhabitants of the world stand in awe of
> Him. for He spoke, and it was done; He commanded,
> and it stood fast. The LORD nullifies the counsel of the
> nations; He frustrates the plans of the peoples. The
> counsel of the LORD stands forever, the plans of His
> heart from generation to generation.[35]

That God is sovereign means that God is King and has
ultimate governance over all creation. God is perfectly free to
direct the universe in any way God chooses. All of creation is
subject to the control of God.

Traditional Baptists and Calvinists do not disagree about
any of this. What they disagree about is what the sovereign
God has decided to do with the world. To put it another way,
they disagree about how God has decided to exercise the
divine sovereignty.

Second, traditional Baptists and Calvinists both believe
that God elects persons. The concept of God choosing persons
is a theme found throughout the Bible. Traditional Baptists
and Calvinists agree that election means that God takes the
initiative in calling persons. In the New Testament God's
basic call is for people to come to Christ. Traditional Baptists

---

[35]Ps. 33:6-11.

agree with Calvinists that it is always God who takes the initiative in salvation. Paul describes Christians as "called to be saints" (Rom. 1:7; 1 Cor. 1:2), and Peter speaks of Christians as those "who are chosen" (1 Pet. 1:1). Traditional Baptists and Calvinists also agree that God calls individuals to specific kinds of service.

Third, traditional Baptists and Calvinists both believe in the love of God. John declares unambiguously that God is love (1 Jn. 4:8, 16). God's love was demonstrated in the sending of Jesus: "For God so loved the world, that He gave His only begotten Son, that whoever believes in Him should not perish, but have eternal life" (Jn. 3:16).

However, even though traditional Baptists and Calvinists both affirm God's love, they understand the nature and extent of God's love differently. Calvinists affirm that God wills for some people—the elect—to be saved but not for all people to be saved. They think that Christ died for the elect and that God gives the gift of faith to the elect. They believe that God passes over the others and allows them to die in their sins even though God might have given them the gift of faith and saved them.

Traditional Baptists do not understand God's love to be discriminating in this way; we believe that God loves everyone and wants everyone to be saved. We believe that God is disappointed by the fact that some people choose to refuse the love and salvation that God through Jesus Christ has offered to all people.[36]

---

[36] 1 Tim. 2:4; 2 Pet. 3:9; Lk. 6:47; 9:24; Acts 7:51; Rev. 22:7.

Fourth, traditional Baptists and Calvinists agree that salvation is by God's grace. People cannot save themselves, and the initiative for salvation lies with God rather than with ourselves. Neither traditional Baptists nor Calvinists are Pelagian. Pelagianism gets its name from a British lay monk who died in the early part of the fifth century. Pelagianism exaggerates the freedom of people and what they are able to achieve. It says that persons are free to obey or disobey God. The Reformed theologian Shirley Guthrie says that Pelagianism

> argues that God has given us laws and command-
> ments to tell us how we must live, and the freedom to
> obey or disobey them. If we choose to obey, God will
> be gracious to us and will help and save us; if we
> refuse to obey, we will get the rejection and pun-
> ishment we deserve. In other words, we save (or
> damn) ourselves by the "good works" we do (or refuse
> to do).[37]

Traditional Baptists reject Pelagianism. With Calvinists we affirm that salvation is by God's grace through faith. Persons cannot save themselves, and they cannot earn salvation. As Paul writes: "For by grace you have been saved through faith; and that not of yourselves, *it is* the gift of God; not as a result of works, so that no one may boast" (Eph. 2:8-9).

---

[37]Shirley Guthrie, *Christian Doctrine*, rev. ed. (Louisville, KY: Westminster/John Knox Press, 1994), 126.

Traditional Baptists and Calvinists agree that salvation is a gift of God's grace; our disagreement is about how God works in grace.

Fifth, traditional Baptists join with Calvinists in affirming the freedom of persons. We both think that freedom means that human beings are not coerced. In describing the theology of Millard Erickson we noted how important human freedom is to him.

But traditional Baptists and Calvinists do not understand human freedom in the same way. Calvinists think that human beings are free to do what they want but that they are not free to want to do good or to accept the gospel. Traditional Baptists believe that human beings are free to choose to do good or evil, and to accept the gospel or to reject it.

Sixth, traditional Baptists and most Calvinists agree that evangelism is important. It is true that the extreme Calvinists, the hyper-Calvinists, do not believe in evangelism. In the nineteenth century Baptists in America were divided over the issue of evangelism and missions when some hyper-Calvinistic Baptists insisted that, since God had predestined some persons to salvation and others to damnation, the church should not engage in evangelism or missions. Fortunately, most of the Calvinists in Baptist life today affirm the mandate to evangelize.

However, traditional Baptists and Calvinists have different motives for evangelism. Traditional Baptists evangelize because we believe that God loves all persons and wants them all to be saved and because we believe that if we will preach the gospel to people they can be saved. Calvinists do not have these motives for evangelism. Their motive for evangelism is simply to be obedient to God's commands to evangelize (Mt. 28:19-20), a motive we share with them.

Now we will examine the biblical passages that, taken at face value, support Calvinism.

5

Scripture: A Calvinist Reading

In this chapter we will survey some of the passages that, taken at face value, provide support for Calvinism. We will not try to cover every passage or to look at each one in detail. Rather we will present the principal passages and state briefly the Calvinist reading of them. In some cases we will also offer a traditional Baptist interpretation.

We will give special attention to passages about God's sovereignty and about predestination because these two issues are so important. Calvinists emphasize the sovereignty of God:

> If God is not sovereign, then he is not God. It belongs to God as God to be sovereign. How we understand his sovereignty has radical implications for our

understanding of the doctrines of providence, election, justification, and a host of others.[38]

Here is a definition of *predestination* from the popular Reformed theologian R. C. Sproul:

> In summary we may define *predestination* broadly as follows: From all eternity God decided to save some members of the human race and to let the rest of the human race perish. God made a choice—he chose some individuals to be saved unto everlasting bless- edness in heaven, and he chose others to pass over, allowing them to suffer the consequences of their sins, eternal punishment in hell.[39]

Old Testament Passages

Calvinists believe that their understanding of election is taught in the Old Testament. They point to the numerous passages that affirm the election of Israel.[40] They emphasize that God chose Israel independently of any merit Israel might have had. They point to numerous Old Testament passages

---

[38] R. C. Sproul, *Grace Unknown: The Heart of Reformed Theology* (Grand Rapids, MI: Baker Books, 1997), 27.

[39]Ibid., 141.

[40]See, for example, Dt. 7:7ff.; Is. 4:8-9; Ezek. 20:5.

that reflect God's call to individual persons.[41] God chose Abel over Cain; God chose Noah over the rest of humanity; God chose Abraham to lead the chosen people over all others; God chose Jacob over his twin Esau; God chose David and his descendants over Saul and his descendants.

Calvinists think that passages such as these, when coupled with the passages that affirm God's sovereignty[42] and humanity's sinfulness,[43] support their belief that God elects and controls persons and situations according to his sovereign will.

Traditional Baptists agree that God chose Israel and also chose certain individuals. In many of these cases God chose people for service rather than for salvation. We do not think that any of these passages suggests that God chose a person to be damned; in the Old Testament as in the New, the decision to reject God's call is made by people, not by God.

Calvinists think that the doctrine of predestination is clarified in the New Testament.

Romans 9

Romans 9 is one of the most important passages in the Bible for Calvinism. Many Calvinists believe that in this

---

[41]See, for example, 1 Sam. 16:1ff.; Is. 45:1ff.; 1 Chr. 28:1ff.

[42]See, for example, Ex. 10:20; 1 Kg. 12:15; Ezra 1:1.

[43]See, for example, Ps. 14:2-3; Jer. 17:9; Pr. 21:1; Is. 46:9-10.

chapter Paul teaches double predestination (God chose some for salvation and some for damnation).

> And not only this, but there was Rebekah also, when she had conceived *twins* by one man, our father Isaac; for though *the twins* were not yet born, and had not done anything good or bad, so that God's purpose according to *His* choice might stand, not because of works but because of Him who calls, it was said to her, "The older will serve the younger." Just as it is written, "Jacob I loved, but Esau I hated."[44]

> So then He has mercy on whom He desires, and He hardens whom He desires.[45]

> Or does not the potter have a right over the clay, to make from the same lump one vessel for honorable use and another for common use? What if God, although willing to demonstrate His wrath and to make His power known, endured with much patience vessels of wrath prepared for destruction? And *He did so* to make known the riches of His glory upon vessels of mercy, which He prepared beforehand for glory, *even* us, whom He also called, not from among Jews only, but also from among Gentiles.[46]

---

[44]Rom. 9:10-13.

[45]Rom. 9:18.

[46]Rom. 9:21-24.

Calvinists say that in this chapter election refers to individuals and not the nation of Israel. They think that Romans 9:24 means that believing Christians are being called from among Jews and Gentiles.

Calvinists also see in these passages an emphasis on human sinfulness. Because of the hardness of human hearts, God turns from them and hardens them in their own sinfulness (Rom. 9:14ff.). At the same time, God reaches out and draws in those chosen from eternity. Calvinists acknowledge that God's eternal choice is a mystery:

> Oh, the depth of the riches both of the wisdom and knowledge of God! How unsearchable are His judgments and unfathomable His ways![47]

In the next chapter we will describe the traditional Baptist interpretation of Romans 9.

Predestination and Foreknowledge

In the New Testament, there are six uses of the Greek word *prohorizo*, which is the word that is translated *predestine*. The word basically means to decide upon something beforehand and thus to predestine it. The important passages for the doctrine of predestination are Romans 8:29-30, 1 Peter 1:1-2, and Ephesians 1:3-12.

In Romans 8:29-30 we read:

---

[47]Rom. 11:33.

For whom He foreknew, He also predestined *to be-come* conformed to the image of His Son, that He would be the firstborn among many brethren; and these whom He predestined, He also called; and these whom He called, He also justified; and these whom He justified, He also glorified.

The Calvinist reading of this passage is that God in eternity chose from humanity a number of persons to be saved and that God's choice was not based on merit or on God's fore-knowledge of future decisions the various persons would make. For Calvinists what God foreknew (v. 29) was not what a person's response to the gospel would be. Rather, according to Calvinists, for God to choose persons before they are born, God must know that they will be born. Thus, the fore-knowledge to which Paul refers in this passage is not a knowledge of future affirmative decisions by the person but simply of the person's future existence. Sproul comments on Romans 8:29:

We notice in this text that God's foreknowledge precedes his predestination. Those who advocate the prescient view [God's foreknowledge of human actions and responses] assume that, since foreknow-ledge precedes predestination, foreknowledge must be the basis of predestination. Paul does not say this. He simply says that God predestined those whom he foreknew. Who else could he possibly predestine? Before God can choose anyone for anything, he must have them in mind as objects of his choice. That Paul links predestination with foreknowledge says nothing about whether this foreknowledge includes the person's meeting some condition for election.[48]

As we will see in the next chapter, traditional Baptists believe that it is important that Paul lists foreknowledge before predestination.

Calvinists understand 1 Peter 1:1-2 to teach their view of predestination:

> Peter, an apostle of Jesus Christ, to those who reside as aliens, scattered throughout Pontus, Galatia, Cappadocia, Asia, and Bithynia, who are chosen according to the foreknowledge of God the Father, by the sanctifying work of the Spirit, to obey Jesus Christ and be sprinkled with His blood: May grace and peace be yours in fullest measure.

Calvinists do not understand this passage to mean that God's predestination of persons is based on foreknowledge of decisions they will make.

Another important passage is Ephesians 1:3-12 where the word *predestine* is used twice:

> Just as He chose us in Him before the foundation of the world, that we should be holy and blameless before Him. In love He predestined us to adoption as

---

[48]Sproul, *Grace Unknown*, 143.

sons through Jesus Christ to Himself, according to the kind intention of His will.[49]

Also we have obtained an inheritance, having been predestined according to His purpose who works all things after the counsel of His will.[50]

Calvinists see these verses as teaching unconditional election by God—God decided in advance who will be saved, and that choice was made irrespective of the human will. In the next chapter we will argue that Paul is here speaking of groups—those who have chosen to be in Christ and those who have refused to be in Christ—rather than of individuals.

Additional Passages

Calvinists use several additional Scriptures to support their doctrine of predestination. Several of the relevant passages appear in John:

"All that the Father gives Me shall come to Me, and the one who comes to Me I will certainly not cast out."[51]

---

[49]Eph. 1:4-5.

[50]Eph. 1:11.

[51]Jn. 6:37.

"No one can come to Me, unless the Father who sent Me draws him; and I will raise him up on the last day."[52]

And He was saying, "For this reason I have said to you, that no one can come to Me unless it has been granted him from the Father."[53]

"You did not choose Me but I chose you, and appointed you, that you would go and bear fruit, and *that* your fruit would remain, so that whatever you ask of the Father in My name He may give to you."[54]

Calvinists believe that these verses teach predestination and irresistible grace. They say that John 6:37 means that a person cannot refuse God's choice of the person. Those given to Christ by God will respond.

Calvinists use John 6:44 and 6:65 to support both predestination and the idea that people are so sinful and depraved that they are unable to turn to God. They think that John 15:16 affirms the secondary status of human choice.

Calvinists think that these passages, taken with the passages in Roman and Ephesians, teach their view of predestination. Many argue that predestination must mean double predestination because one cannot come to Christ unless one

---

[52]Jn. 6:44.

[53]Jn. 6:65.

[54]Jn. 15:16.

has been predestined by God, and God allows those who are not elected to die under the divine judgment.

Here are five other New Testament passages that are important in Calvinism.

When the Gentiles heard this, they *began* rejoicing and glorifying the word of the Lord; and as many as had been appointed to eternal life believed.[55]

But when God who had set me apart *even* from my mother's womb and called me through His grace, was pleased to reveal His Son in me so that I might preach Him among the Gentiles, I did not immediately consult with flesh and blood.[56]

But we should always give thanks to God for you, brethren beloved by the Lord, because God has chosen you from the beginning for salvation through sanctification by the Spirit and faith in the truth.[57]

And, "A stone of stumbling and a rock of offense"; for they stumble because they are disobedient to the word, and to this *doom* they were also appointed.[58]

---

[55] Acts 13:48.

[56] Gal. 1:15-16.

[57] 2 Th. 2:13.

[58] 1 Pet. 2:8.

For certain persons have crept in unnoticed, those who
were long beforehand marked out for this condemnation, ungodly persons who turn the grace of our
God into licentiousness and deny our only Master and
Lord, Jesus Christ.[59]

Calvinists find predestination in all of these passages. They
believe that the description of Paul's experience given in
Galatians 1:15-16 means that God had predestined Paul
before his birth and that God's grace on his life was irresistible, and they think that what was true of Paul is true also of
all Christians. Some Calvinists think that 1 Peter 2:8 teaches
that God has predestined some people to hell.

Conclusion

A survey of these passages reveals that one reading—in
several cases a reading at face value—supports the Calvinistic
doctrine of predestination. But we ask: Is this the only reading
of these passages? Is it the best reading? Does this reading
incorporate the whole of Scripture? As traditional Baptists we
think the answer to these questions is No. We believe that
there is another, better way to understand these passages.

---

[59]Jude 1:4.

6

Scripture: A Traditional Baptist Reading

Our purpose in this chapter is to give a traditional Baptist reading of Scripture in general and of passages about predestination in particular. This will involve examining some of the passages reviewed in the previous chapter as well as looking at some other passages.

The Love of God

We begin with a passage that guides us as traditional Baptists to believe that God loves all people.

> For God so loved the world, that He gave His only begotten Son, that whoever believes in Him should not perish, but have eternal life.[60]

---

[60]Jn. 3:16.

We believe that, because God loves all people, God wants all people to be saved.

> "Say to them, 'As I live!'" declares the Lord GOD, "I take no pleasure in the death of the wicked, but rather that the wicked turn from his way and live. Turn back, turn back from your evil ways! Why then will you die, O house of Israel?"[61]

> [God] desires all men to be saved and to come to the knowledge of the truth.[62]

> The Lord is not slow about His promise, as some count slowness, but is patient toward you, not wishing for any to perish but for all to come to repentance.[63]

God loves every person and for that reason wants every person to be saved. God offers salvation to all people, and they are able to accept or to reject God's offer. Because we believe so deeply in the biblical teaching about God's love for all people, we think it is best to understand the passages about predestination in the light of God's love for all people.

One of the ways that the Bible displays God's love for all persons is to say that Christ died for all persons.

---

[61]Ezek. 33:11.

[62]1 Tim. 2:4.

[63]2 Pet. 3:9.

All of us like sheep have gone astray, each of us has turned to his own way; but the LORD has caused the iniquity of us all to fall on Him.[64]

Come to Me, all who are weary and heavy-laden, and I will give you rest.[65]

[Jesus] gave Himself as a ransom for all.[66]

For it is for this we labor and strive, because we have fixed our hope on the living God, who is the Savior of all men, especially of believers.[67]

For the grace of God has appeared, bringing salvation to all men.[68]

But we do see Him who has been made for a little while lower than the angels, *namely,* Jesus, because of the suffering of death crowned with glory and honor, so that by the grace of God He might taste death for everyone.[69]

---

[64]Is. 53:6.

[65]Mt. 11:28.

[66]1 Tim. 2:6.

[67]1 Tim. 4:10.

[68]Titus 2:11.

[69]Heb. 2:9.

He [Jesus] Himself is the propitiation for our sins; and not for ours only, but also for *those of* the whole world.[70]

Calvinists think that in these verses the words "the world" and "all" refer to the elect only. Traditional Baptists think it is best to accept these words at face value. When the Scripture says that Christ died for all we believe that it means just that, and when the Scripture says that Christ died for the sins of the world, we believe that it means just that.

This does not mean that all persons receive the benefit of Christ's death. Traditional Baptists believe that Christ died for all but that salvation is given only to those who receive it by faith. This is what Paul was saying in 1 Timothy 4:10. The free offer of salvation is extended to everyone, but it is given only to those who accept it in faith.

Calvinists say that the invitation to Christ is given universally, but only those who are predestined are able to respond. We think that this reading misses the point of the passages quoted above. God loves all the world; Christ died for all the world; God desires that all the people in the world receive Christ as Savior. If some do not receive Christ, it is not because God has not given them the ability to have faith but rather because they have chosen to reject Christ.

---

[70] 1 Jn. 2:2.

The Gift of Freedom

Human freedom is a debated issue in discussions of predestination. Calvinists argue that the freedom of a person to accept or reject Christ is contradictory to the sovereignty of God. They either deny that human beings are free or offer a severely restricted understanding of human freedom. But our reading of Scripture is that the freedom of persons to respond to God is sometimes clearly affirmed in the Bible and, even more frequently, is assumed by the writers of the Bible.

The story of Adam and Eve was written on the assumption that they were given the freedom to say Yes to God or to say No.[71]

The ability to choose is implied in passages where a call to respond is issued. Moses attempted to convince Israel that God wanted to lead them out of Egypt on the assumption that they could decide whether or not to follow (Ex. 4:1-9). Moses led the Israelites in the wilderness for forty years to see whether the people of God would keep the commandments of God—the choice was theirs.[72] Later the Israelites were in a situation where they could change their minds (Ex. 13:7).

Joshua called upon the people to "choose for yourselves today whom you will serve."[73]

The prophets of Israel issued repeated calls to the people to repent on the assumption the people of Israel could and

---

[71]See Genesis 3.

[72]Dt. 8:2; see also Dt. 13:1-3; Jg. 2:22; 3:4; Ex. 16:4.

[73]Josh. 24:15.

must make their own decision. Jeremiah believed that the people could choose how they would respond to the Word of the Lord (Jer. 22:1-3). Even the parable of the potter, in which the emphasis falls more on God's sovereignty than on the human response to God, includes the call: "Thus says the LORD, 'Behold, I am fashioning calamity against you and devising a plan against you. Oh turn back, each of you from his evil way, and reform your ways and your deeds" (Jer. 18:11). Throughout the Scripture there is a continual call to the people to believe:

> "Come now, and let us reason together," says the LORD, "Though your sins are as scarlet, They will be as white as snow; though they are red like crimson, they will be like wool. If you consent and obey, you will eat the best of the land; but if you refuse and rebel, you will be devoured by the sword." Truly, the mouth of the LORD has spoken.[74]

The same emphasis appears in the New Testament. Throughout his ministry and teaching Jesus assumed that people were free to accept or to reject his message. The theme of his ministry is proclaimed at the beginning: "Repent, for the kingdom of heaven is at hand" (Mt. 4:17). His call to his disciples to follow him (Mt. 4:19) was a call they could either accept or reject. In his teaching regarding Christian living Jesus assumed that his listeners would be able to choose whether to obey or disobey him. Jesus had numerous en-

---

[74]Is. 1:18-20.

counters with real people who made choices: Nicodemus (Jn. 3:1-12), the Samaritan woman (Jn. 4:1-26), the lame man (Jn. 5:1-8), the woman caught in adultery (Jn. 7:53-8:11), the man born blind (Jn. 9:1-7), the rich young ruler (Lk. 18:18-25), and Zacchaeus (Lk. 19:1-10). In the biblical accounts of these encounters it is assumed that the persons chose how they would respond to Jesus.

Further, many of Jesus' parables include a call to decision. The parables call us to think and to decide. Will we be the good soil? How will we use our talents? Have we counted the cost? Are we neighbors to those in need? Will we return to the Father like the lost son? Are we prepared for the coming crisis? Are we ready for the judgment? Are we sheep or goats? Jesus constantly called his listeners to make choices.

Jesus' commission to the church to share the gospel was given on the assumption that people have the ability to say Yes or No to God's call (Mt. 28:19-20; Acts 1:8).

Another group of passages in which it is assumed that people have the ability to respond to the gospel are the sermons recorded in Acts. Peter preached on the Day of Pentecost and called upon the hearers to repent (Acts 2:30), presumably on the assumption that they could repent if they chose to do so. When he preached to the crowd outside the Beautiful Gate at the temple he again called for repentance (Acts 3:19; see also 13:38). Repentance basically means to change one's mind. It includes an element of changing one's life. The call to repentance is a call to turn from one way of living to another.

Several passages in Acts contain invitations for people to have faith in God (Acts 6:43, 16:31). Our English word "believe" can cause us to miss the biblical meaning of "faith." Paul's response to the Philippian jailer's question, "What must I do to be saved?" was, "Believe in the Lord Jesus, and you shall be saved" (Acts 16:31). The word translated "believe" is the verb form of the noun which is translated "faith." The biblical meaning is clearer if we say that Paul told the jailor to "faith the Lord Jesus." It is not good English grammar to use "faith" as a verb, but it is good theology. Faith includes trust, confidence, and decision, and is connected to obedience. It is God's will for people to respond to the gospel by putting their faith in Jesus. Frank Stagg comments:

> In one sense, faith is God's gift, yet it must be a gift received. In Ephesians 2:8 the "gift of God" probably refers to salvation rather than to faith; but in Philippians 1:29 "to trust" (*pisteuein*) is clearly the gift of grace (*echaristhē*). Man could not trust if God did not offer himself to man; but trust is never coercive. Faith is the response of trust to God's gracious self-giving. It is openness of heart, mind, and life to God. It is an openness to God to receive what he has to give and to yield what he demands.[75]

Paul declared that faith has its beginning with the hearing of the gospel (Rom. 10:12-17). Faith and repentance are responses that a sinner makes to God. Although human beings

---

[75]Frank Stagg, *New Testament Theology* (Nashville: Broadman Press, 1962), 120.

are helpless before God and powerless to redeem themselves, God has created them with the capacity to respond to the offer of saving grace either positively or negatively. God elicits the human response of faith by sending his Son Jesus, but faith is a response that humans themselves must make. Though Paul was not talking about the initial experience of salvation at the time, he makes a similar emphasis in Romans 8:28 when he says that God works for good with those that love God. Likewise, in Philippians 2:13 Paul says: "For it is God who is at work in you, both to will and to work for *His* good pleasure." Paul admonished the church at Ephesus, "And do not grieve the Holy Spirit of God" (Eph. 4:30). The writer of Hebrews exhorted his readers not to harden their hearts (Heb. 3:8, 15; 4:7). There is no indication in these texts that the persons are anything but free to choose.

In saying that people are free to choose whether or not to put their faith in Christ, we do not mean that faith is a good work or that we contribute anything to our salvation. When we exercise faith, we are not earning credit with God. Faith is not a way of saving ourselves. It is simply our affirmative response of trusting God and accepting the wonderful salvation that Christ provided. Paul writes: "For by grace you have been saved through faith; and that not of yourselves, *it is* the gift of God; not as a result of works, that no one should boast" (Eph. 2:8-9). This means that God's salvation is a gift that we receive by trusting in Christ; that is our response to God's initiative in Christ. In Christ God accomplishes salvation and offers it to us; we simply receive it; we contribute nothing to it. It is the gift of God.

Traditional Baptists agree with Calvinists that God had the power and the knowledge to arrange things so that after human beings had sinned they would be unable to make the kind of positive response to the gospel that we have been describing. After all, God is sovereign. But we think that the Scripture teaches that God in fact chose to do things differently than Calvinists say. Scripture teaches that God created human beings with the freedom to respond positively or negatively to the offer of salvation in Christ and that freedom was not destroyed by their fall into sin. God sovereignly delegated to each of us the choice about how we would respond to Christ.

Though our concern here is not with why God created human beings with freedom, a comment by C. S. Lewis may be helpful to those pondering the question:

> Why, then, did God give them free will? Because free will, though it makes evil possible, is also the only thing that makes possible any love or goodness or joy worth having. A world of automata—of creatures that worked like machines—would hardly be worth creating.[76]

---

[76]C. S. Lewis, *Mere Christianity* (New York: Macmillan, 1952), 52.

God's Sovereignty and Human Freedom

Calvinists think that it would limit God if human beings were free, that human freedom in the sense we described above is somehow contradictory to the sovereignty of God. But the biblical writers apparently did not feel that divine sovereignty and human freedom were contradictory, for throughout the Bible they affirm them side by side without any attempt to explain them. We will examine numerous passages in which they did this.

The story of the potter and the clay in Jeremiah 18 emphasizes both themes. The sovereignty of God is found in vv. 7-10:

> At one moment I [God] might speak concerning a nation or concerning a kingdom to uproot, to pull down, or to destroy *it;* if that nation against which I have spoken turns from its evil, I will relent concerning the calamity I planned to bring on it. Or at another moment I might speak concerning a nation or concerning a kingdom to build up or to plant *it;* if it does evil in My sight by not obeying My voice, then I will think better of the good with which I had promised to bless it.

This is followed immediately by the assertion that the nations have the option to change. God is in control; persons must decide. Both truths are affirmed.

Several passages that refer to Christ's death do so by speaking of both the sovereignty of God and the freedom of persons. Peter's sermon in Acts 2 is one example:

> Men of Israel, listen to these words: Jesus the Nazarene, a man attested to you by God with miracles and wonders and signs which God performed through Him in your midst, just as you yourselves know–this *Man,* delivered over by the predetermined plan and foreknowledge of God, you nailed to a cross by the hands of godless men and put *Him* to death.[77]

God controls the final outcome, but those who crucified Jesus are held accountable for their actions. The same dual emphasis is found in another of his sermons:

> The God of Abraham, Isaac, and Jacob, the God of our fathers, has glorified His servant Jesus, *the one* whom you delivered up, and disowned in the presence of Pilate, when he had decided to release Him. But you disowned the Holy and Righteous One, and asked for a murderer to be granted to you, but put to death the Prince of life, *the one* whom God raised from the dead, *a fact* to which we are witnesses.[78]

In Acts 4:24-30 after Peter and John were released from prison the church prayed a prayer that emphasized God's

---

[77] Acts 2:22-23.

[78] Acts 3:13-15.

sovereignty (vv. 24-26) in the matter of Jesus' death, but at the same time they recognized the role of Judas.

Jesus himself spoke of his death as being part of God's sovereign plan and also the result of evil choices by human beings:

> For this reason the Father loves Me, because I lay down My life so that I may take it again. No one has taken it away from Me, but I lay it down on My own initiative. I have authority to lay it down, and I have authority to take it up again. This commandment I received from My Father.[79]

> You would have no authority over Me, unless it had been given you from above; for this reason he who delivered Me up to you has *the* greater sin.[80]

Several passages in the Gospel of John illustrate the proper relationship between the sovereignty of God and the freedom of persons.[81] Let us examine a few of those passages, with particular reference to those passages often cited by Calvinists. In John 1:9-13 we read:

---

[79]Jn. 10:17-18.

[80]Jn. 19:11.

[81]For a more detailed discussion see Grant R. Osborne, "Soteriology in the Gospel of John" in *The Grace of God and the Will of Man*, ed. Clark H. Pinnock (Minneapolis: Bethany House Publishers, 1989).

There was the true Light which, coming into the world, enlightens every man. . . . He came to His own, and those who were His own did not receive Him. But as many as received Him, to them He gave the right to become children of God, *even* to those who believe in His name, who were born, not of blood nor of the will of the flesh nor of the will of man, but of God.

Becoming children of God is an act of God; yet everyone who is exposed to the light has the responsibility to reject or accept it. John asserts that all persons are enlightened: some reject the light that is Jesus, and others accept Jesus. When they accept Jesus, God effects a new birth in them.

The discussion in John 6:22-50 has a strong emphasis on God's sovereign control of salvation. But just a few verses later responsibility and sovereignty are intertwined.

Jesus said to them, "I am the bread of life; he who comes to Me will not hunger, and he who believes in Me will never thirst. But I said to you, that you have seen Me, and yet do not believe. All that the Father gives Me shall come to Me, and the one who comes to Me I will certainly not cast out."[82]

Jesus asserts that those who come to him and believe in him will have life. Those who disbelieve are held accountable for their decisions. On the other hand, there is also an emphasis on the life that is given by the Father. This passage affirms

---

[82]Jn. 6:35-37.

God's election in that God chooses before we choose. But we believe that the passage supports the belief that God works with faith rather than that God works in the lives of some people by an irresistible grace that produces faith.

In John 6:44 Jesus said, "No one can come to Me, unless the Father who sent Me draws him; and I will raise him up on the last day." This same emphasis is repeated in John 6:65: "And He was saying, 'For this reason I have said to you, that no one can come to Me unless it has been granted him from the Father.'" The Calvinist reading of these verses is that God's drawing controls the response of the person, but we think that Jesus is assuming that God draws all people, not just some. John 12:12 is our clue for this: Jesus said that he would "draw all men" to himself.

John's emphasis seems clear enough—God is in control of salvation. God takes the initiative. God calls. God draws. But the reason that some are not included is not that God has not called them but rather that they have rejected God's call.

The dual emphasis is found in John 10 also. Jesus is the Good Shepherd who knows his sheep. Verses 27-29 are a declaration of security to the sheep that are in God's hand. Election is sure, but the text does not suggest that election produces faith; rather it works alongside faith. This is seen in vv. 33-39 where Jesus calls the very ones he had just addressed to a faith response: "If I do not do the works of My Father, do not believe Me; but if I do them, though you do not believe Me, believe the works, so that you may know and understand that the Father is in Me, and I in the Father" (Jn. 10:37-38). Their response speaks for itself: "And many believed in Him there" (Jn. 10:42).

We have examined just a few of the many passages in John. An emphasis on both the sovereignty of God and the faith-decision is, however, seen throughout the book. Grant Osborne, after a thorough examination of all the passages in John, commented:

> For John, election is a reality; those who are Jesus' followers have been chosen and given to Christ. Their salvation is not due to their own efforts, for as part of the world, they once were totally depraved, in complete rebellion against God and without hope. Their conversion was an act of God, achieved through their encounter with Christ. Yet, at the same time they came to Christ by way of faith-decision; they saw, believed, and thus knew Jesus as their Savior. Moreover, Christ came not just for the elect, but as the "light of the world" and as "savior of the world." All people are equally drawn to the Father. . . . God is an "equal opportunity" convicter who, in drawing all to himself, makes it possible to make a true decision to accept or reject Jesus. Those who accept are "chosen" and "given" to Christ. That decision is not possible without God's drawing power but it is a free moral decision with irresistible coercion. Election is still theologically true but is not absolute, i.e., apart from man's decision.[83]

---

[83] Osborne, "Soteriology," 256-57.

Romans 9–11

Interpreters agree that Romans 9–11 stands together as a unit. In these chapters the general concern that Paul was addressing was why so few Jews were being saved when so many Gentiles were being saved. For Paul this problem had three dimensions. It was a personal problem; he was distressed that so few of his fellow Jews were being converted (Rom. 9:3-4; 10:1). It was also a theological problem; if, as Paul believed, Christ is the fulfillment of promises that God gave to the Jews but not to the Gentiles, then it was very difficult to understand why so few Jews were being saved and so many Gentiles were being saved. It was also a church problem; some in the church at Rome seem to have harbored some anti-Jewish sentiments, which Paul attacked (Rom. 11:13-24).

Paul makes several points in these chapters. First, though some Israelites reject God, this does not negate God's righteousness (ch. 9). Second, the righteous God has chosen to be merciful even to those who disobey (ch. 10). Third, though many Gentiles are now accepting the gospel, in the end some will not and thus they will be lost; whereas many Jews are now rejecting the gospel, but in the end some will accept the gospel and thus they will be saved (ch. 11).

Paul begins by stating the fact that though so few of his fellow Jews are being saved, this does not constitute a failure of the sovereignty of God. But when Paul writes that "God has mercy on whom he wants to have mercy, and he hardens whom he wants to harden" (Rom. 9:18), he is not talking about salvation; he is talking about God's choice of Israel to be the bearer of God's love. God's choice of Jacob over Esau is the choice of a people through whom God would work. Similarly, verse 13 at face value suggests that God literally hates the person Esau. But we think that Paul meant that God rejected Esau not as a person but as the one who would play a special role in the work of God in the world. One reason we think this is that Paul was writing about Jews who believed that they were a special people due not only to God's call but also to their birth and merit. Paul shows that their selection through Jacob was before his birth and without merit.

As we observed earlier, Calvinists point to Romans 9:22-23 as evidence of God's predestination:

> What if God, although willing to demonstrate His wrath and to make His power known, endured with much patience vessels of wrath prepared for destruction? And *He did so* to make known the riches of His glory upon vessels of mercy, which He prepared beforehand for glory.

Calvinists read this to mean that one's destiny has been decided in advance by God. We agree that Paul is affirming God's power and authority to determine, but we think that he is actually affirming that God did not in fact choose to respond that way. Rather, God "endured with much patience" (9:22) persons whose lives are fit for destruction. Paul is not saying that God determined that they are to be that way; rather

God endures patiently those who choose the way of destruction.[84]

Paul goes on to say that the reason that Israel was not being saved is that Israel was rejecting the good news (Rom. 10:16). But then Paul adds that some of Israel was being saved, a faithful remnant, and Paul himself was among that remnant (Rom. 11:1-5).

In chapter 11 Paul made a comment that is puzzling but is surely relevant to this matter: "All Israel will be saved" (Rom. 11:26). There are various ways to interpret this verse. Perhaps it is best to begin by remembering Paul's passionate concern for his fellow Jews—he is distressed that so many Jews are not believing in Jesus. In that context Paul's emphasis seems to be that salvation is still possible for Jews. "All Israel" probably refers to all the believing Israelites. Such an interpretation is consistent with Paul's argument in Romans 9:6 that not all those born Israelites are true Israelites in the faith. All Israelites who trust in Jesus Christ are recipients of God's grace.

---

[84] For more discussion of these texts see Dale Moody, "Romans" in *The Broadman Bible Commentary*, vol. 10 (Nashville: Broadman Press, 1970), 231-32 and Herschel H. Hobbs, *Romans* (Waco, TX: Word Books, Publisher, 1977), 127. Both discuss the fact that the Greek participle rendered "made for" could be middle or passive voice. If Paul intended the middle voice, then the idea is that persons have made themselves for destruction. If Paul intended the passive voice, the idea is that they have been created for destruction. Both Moody and Hobbs prefer the former.

Paul offered a complex interpretation of what he was observing in his work as a missionary. He said that Gentiles who were once disobedient have received God's mercy as a result of the disobedience of the Jews, and similarly Jews will now receive mercy as a result of God's mercy to the Gentiles. Then he added, "For God has bound all men over to disobedience so that he may have mercy on them all" (Rom. 11:32). As Paul reflected on all this he confessed that what God is doing is mysterious and that people cannot understand it. He then concluded by praising God.

> Oh, the depth of the riches both of the wisdom and knowledge of God! How unsearchable are His judgments and unfathomable His ways! . . . From Him and through Him and to Him are all things. To Him *be* the glory forever. Amen.[85]

Traditional Baptists agree with Calvinists that Romans 9 is about God's election or predestination of Israel. But throughout much of these three chapters Paul is asserting that predestination is more about Israel's call to serve the Gentiles than about Israel's salvation. The entire matter is a mystery known only to God.

In view of the message of all three chapters it seems best to understand the claims of chapter 9 not in Calvinistic terms but along these lines: God is in charge, and even though right now we cannot understand everything that God is doing, we

---

[85]Rom. 11:33-36.

know that God will make everything turn out all right in the end.

Foreknowledge and Predestination

We come now to our final set of passages, those that speak directly of foreknowledge and predestination.

In Romans 8:29-30 Paul relates predestination to foreknowledge.

> For whom He foreknew, He also predestined *to become* conformed to the image of His Son, so that He would be the firstborn among many brethren; and these whom He predestined, He also called; and these whom He called, He also justified; and these whom He justified, He also glorified.

Traditional Baptists believe that it is significant that in this passage God's foreknowledge precedes God's work of predestination. We understand this to mean that God foresaw the decisions of those who would respond to the gospel and predestined them to be saved. Traditional Baptists have been willing to live with the tension that God foreknows our decisions and at the same time we are free to make decisions. Paul expresses this tension in Galatians 4:8-9:

> However at that time, when you did not know God, you were slaves to those which by nature are no gods.

But now that you have come to know God, or rather to be known by God, how is it that you turn back again to the weak and worthless elemental things, to which you desire to be enslaved all over again?

Freedom and foreknowledge function side by side.

A second observation about Romans 8:28-29 is that there is another way of understanding predestination here than in reference to salvation. We think that what Paul is affirming in this particular passage is that God predestined that Christians will be conformed to "the image of his Son" (v. 29) or become Christlike (see also 2 Cor. 3:18) rather than that God predestined that those who trust Christ will be saved. "Predestined" in these verses might best be translated "marked out beforehand" as a way of indicating that those who are foreknown by God are marked out to be made in the likeness of Jesus.

Another passage that we looked at earlier was Ephesians1:4-6.

Just as He chose us in Him before the foundation of the world, that we should be holy and blameless before Him. In love He predestined us to adoption as sons through Jesus Christ to Himself, according to the kind intention of His will, to the praise of the glory of His grace, which He freely bestowed on us in the Beloved.

In this passage it is Christ who is the Chosen One of God, and, because believers corporately participate in Christ, they are chosen also. Verses 5-6 are not about the predestination of an individual's salvation. Rather, Paul is saying that God has predestined that those who believe will be glorified. Christ is predestined for glory, so we who are in Christ are predestined for glory too. The phrase "in Christ" or its equivalent occurs ten times in Ephesians 1. When Paul says, "In love He predestined us," the "us" refers to believers. And, of course, in verse 13 Paul emphasizes the human choice to believe in Christ: "In Him, you also, after listening to the message of truth, the gospel of your salvation—having also believed."

Paul's point is profound yet simple: Before the foundation of the world God predestined that the way of salvation was in Christ. God's provision of salvation is no accident. It is not by chance that we are God's children—it was God's plan from the beginning that persons who trusted in Christ would experience salvation. Just as we have seen in other passages, we are reminded that God is the Sovereign One who saves sinners who are in Christ.

Conclusion

Both traditional Baptists and Calvinists believe that their views are taught in the Bible. This is because there are two sets of passages in the Bible. One of these sets, taken at face value, supports traditional Baptist theology; the other, taken at face value, supports Calvinism. We are guided to take the first set of passages at face value by our conviction that one of the most fundamental Christian teachings is that God loves all people. Then, because we believe that the biblical message is consistent, we interpret the passages that seem at face value to teach Calvinism, in light of those that teach the traditional Baptist view; in particular, we interpret them in light of the teaching of John 3:16 that God loves everyone in the world.

Guided by this principle, we find that the Bible teaches a doctrine of election that affirms that salvation is a work of God in which God takes the initiative and that God's initiative elicits a response of faith from us. God loved us and called us before we ever responded. We believe that election is in Christ. Apart from Christ there is no salvation. We believe that election is not coercion. We believe that election is purposeful. God desires that all those in Christ be Christlike and that part of being Christlike is to share the Good News with all the world, for God truly desires that all the world come to be a part of the family of God.

7

Traditional Baptist Theology

In this chapter we will describe the traditional Baptist understanding of God's sovereignty and our salvation. Traditional Baptist theology is not simply an alternative to Calvinism; it is an affirmation of many important doctrines concerning God, salvation, and ourselves.

The Sovereignty of God and Predestination

Traditional Baptists believe that God is the all-wise, all-powerful Creator of the world and therefore the absolute, sovereign Lord of all the universe. On the sovereignty of God traditional Baptists agree with Calvinism.

But we disagree with Calvinism in our understanding of what God does with that sovereignty. We believe that before the world began God sovereignly decided—or decreed, planned, willed, foreordained —to create human beings with personal freedom. In deciding to create free human beings God did not lose control of the universe. What God did was to decide to be the sovereign Lord of a universe that is populated with human beings who have freedom.

Because God created human beings with personal freedom, they are able to make real choices. It is God's will for them to have the ability to make real choices. However, human beings sometimes exercise that God-given ability and choose to do things that are contrary to God's will for them. When human beings choose to disobey God, they are not doing something that God decreed or willed or planned or foreordained but are acting contrary to God's will. When they do this God remains the sovereign Lord both in the sense that God's initial will—to create free human beings—is being carried out and in the sense that God never loses control of the course of human history or of the universe. God remains sovereign over a world in which free human beings are acting contrary to the will of God.

Traditional Baptists believe that, before the creation of the world, God knew that human beings would choose to be disobedient. Further, God decided—foreordained, decreed, willed, planned—to respect the decisions that human beings make. By *respect the decisions* we mean that in sovereignly deciding to create human beings with the ability to be obedient or disobedient, God also sovereignly decided to respond to their decisions in appropriate ways, that is, to respond to the good decisions that human beings make with approval and to respond to the evil decisions that human beings make with disapproval.

Perhaps that is putting it too gently, for God's response to sin includes that those who commit sin should be condemned, suffer, and die. This was a righteous decision, of course. It also was inevitable because God created human beings so that they can experience their true destiny of divine approval and happiness and life only in fellowship with God, never in rebellion against God.

Traditional Baptists believe that God sovereignly decided to respond to human rebellion in another way also, in a way that was generous and gracious, namely, by forgiving sinners and rescuing them from their sin. God decided that Jesus Christ would make provision for the salvation of sinners and that he would do so at great personal sacrifice. Forgiveness was costly to God.

Traditional Baptists believe that God sovereignly decided that the followers of Jesus would preach the gospel of Jesus to all the world. God decided that those who accept the gospel would be saved—they are the elect—and that those who reject the gospel would be lost—they are the reprobate. God did not decide which individuals would make which response, only that those who made the different responses would experience different destinies.

Traditional Baptists believe that God sovereignly decided to take many specific initiatives toward human beings. One of these initiatives was to create a people of God's own, and God decided that the Jews—the descendants of Abraham and Sarah—were to be those people. God also decided to call certain individuals to play special roles in carrying out God's work in the world, and God decided that Paul would be one of the these individuals. These decisions of God were a foreordination to service rather than of predestination to salvation or to condemnation. Traditional Baptists believe that the decision about whether or not an individual is saved is a decision that the individual makes, not God, for God's will is that all individuals be saved.

These are the principal things that traditional Baptists believe about God's sovereignty, and they can be summarized in five sentences about God's will. We believe that from eternity it was God's will that people live righteous lives and be happy and not be condemned and not die. We also believe that from eternity it was God's will that people who sinned would experience the consequences of their sin, namely, suffering, death, and condemnation. Further, it was God's will to provide salvation for sinners and to do this through his Son Jesus Christ. And from eternity it was God's will for the followers of Jesus to proclaim the message of salvation and that those who accept the gospel would be saved and that those who reject it would be lost. We also believe that from eternity it was God's will that the nation of Israel and selected individuals such as Paul would play special roles in carrying out God's work in the world.

The God of traditional Baptist theology is a sovereign God whose wisdom and power are such that God might have decided to do what Calvinists say God did, namely, predestine some individuals to salvation and others to damnation. But traditional Baptists believe that God sovereignly decided to act otherwise and to do the things we have described instead.

The Knowledge of God

Traditional Baptists believe that God has all knowledge and all wisdom and all understanding. God's knowledge includes a knowledge of the future. God's foreknowledge is a mysterious matter, and traditional Baptists do not claim to understand it. They believe it because it is taught in the Bible.

Many traditional Baptists are aware that various proposals have been made concerning God's foreknowledge. For example, it has been proposed that God's foreknowledge is an infinitely great version of the limited kind of foreknowledge that human beings have. We human beings know, for example, that if we fall asleep while driving we will wreck our cars. It is natural for us to think about God's foreknowledge as being like this, only infinitely greater and more certain.

Traditional Baptists also are familiar with a second proposal concerning foreknowledge, namely, that, since God inhabits eternity rather than time,[86] God is outside of time and thus timeless, with the result that God knows all past and future events as present events while being aware that human beings are experiencing these as past or future events. This is a very mysterious claim, one whose meaning is unclear to many traditional Baptists; some traditional Baptists have embraced it as a suitable understanding of God's foreknowledge, but others have not. C. S. Lewis, an Anglican who believed that God's eternality makes God's fore-

---

[86]Is. 57:15.

knowledge possible, said that this idea is not taught in the Bible.[87]

Many traditional Baptists are familiar with a third idea, namely, the Calvinistic proposal that God knows the future because God has foreordained everything that will happen in the future. As we have seen, traditional Baptists reject this proposal.

Of course, traditional Baptists do accept a limited version of this proposal, one that says that God foreordains some things in the future and so foreknows them. We have seen that traditional Baptists believe that God foreordained that Jesus would be the Savior and that the Jews and certain individuals such as Paul would have special roles to play in the carrying out of God's work in the world. Naturally, since God had decided to do these things, God foreknew that they would happen.

Some traditional Baptists are familiar with a fourth idea concerning foreknowledge, namely, the proposal that there are future events that God does not know because God cannot know them, but very few traditional Baptists accept this proposal. The argument for this proposal is as follows. We believe that God is all-powerful. Nevertheless, we realize that there are some things that God cannot do; God cannot make a circle with three sides, and God cannot make a rock so big that God can't pick it up. The fact that God cannot do things such as these does not constitute a limitation of God's power; the things are simply self-contradictory. Therefore the wisest way to speak of God's power is to say, not that God can do all

---

[87]C. S. Lewis, *Mere Christianity*, 145-49.

things, but that God can do all things that are doable. That is the most accurate description of divine omnipotence.

There is, the argument goes, a parallel between God's power and God's knowledge, so something similar needs to be said about omniscience: God can know all things that are knowable. Just as there are some things that are not doable, so there are some things that are not knowable. The former do not constitute a limitation of God's power, and the latter do not constitute a limitation of God's knowledge. It has been proposed that real chance in the world, which philosophers call *contingency*, and that really free decisions by human beings, are things that are not knowable, in the same way that making a circle with sides is not doable. The reason that contingency and free choices are not knowable is that in an important sense they do not yet exist. A further idea that makes this plausible is that it is difficult to understand how God could know everything in the future without having determined in advance everything that will occur.

Very few traditional Baptists accept this proposal; most believe that God foreknows everything that will happen. Of course, they quickly add that this does not mean that God has predetermined everything that will happen.

Most traditional Baptists probably accept one of the first two explanations of foreknowledge while at the same time confessing that God's foreknowledge is a mysterious matter. They believe in God's foreknowledge without understanding it, but they are sure that, however foreknowledge works, God does not predestine everything that will happen.

That is our understanding also. God foreknows the future, but how God does this is a mystery. We are open to the idea that God's foreknowledge bears some resemblance to the way in which human beings know very limited things about the future, but of course God's knowledge is infinitely greater and more certain and, indeed, infallible. That God is eternal might mean that in some sense God knows the past and the future as present, though we find this idea extremely obscure; so far as we are aware, no writer in the Bible explained God's foreknowledge by appealing to the fact that God is eternal. We believe that in some cases God has decided to do certain things in the future—to send Christ and to call the Jews and to commission certain individuals to special service—but we see no biblical justification for the claim that God has decided in advance everything that will happen. We believe that God has not foreordained or decreed or willed everything that will happen because among the many things that happen human beings sin, and we do not believe that sin is ever God's will but is rather contrary to it. We believe that God foreknew that human beings would sin, but not that God willed or decided or decreed or foreordained or predestined that they would do so.

Human Freedom

Traditional Baptists believe that God sovereignly decided to create human beings with personal freedom and to respect the decisions they make.

In a sense this freedom seems to limit God's sovereignty, in that human beings are free to decide to disobey the commands of God. But in another and more important sense human freedom is no limitation upon God's sovereignty because, first, it was God's sovereign decision that human beings be free, and, second, it was God's sovereign decision to respect the decisions that people make. In other words, God sovereignly gives humans freedom and sovereignly permits them to sin. But God does not will that they sin.

Concerning the much-discussed question of the relation of God's sovereignty to human freedom, we think that it is not necessary to choose which is real because both are real. We also think that it is not necessary to discuss which is dominant because it seems clear to us that the sovereign God is dominant; freedom is a gift that the sovereign God has given to human beings.

We also believe that it is not difficult to know whether divine sovereignty or human freedom is religiously more important. Divine sovereignty is religiously more important; if God were not the sovereign Lord of the universe, Christianity as we know it would be mistaken. God is the sovereign Lord.

Nevertheless the freedom of human beings also is religiously important. We think that the difficulty of reconciling God's sovereignty and human freedom arises only if one assumes in advance that divine sovereignty means that God wills or foreordains or decrees everything that will happen in the world. As we have said repeatedly, we believe that God might have exercised sovereignty in this way but chose rather to exercise it by giving human beings freedom and then respecting the decisions they make even when those decisions are contrary to God's will.

Sin

Traditional Baptists believe that human beings were created in God's image; that was God's will for them. But human beings chose to disobey God, and sin became embedded in their lives. All human life, both personal and social, has been affected by sin.

We believe that human beings are powerless to save themselves from sin. They do not have the power to forgive themselves for their disobedience to God; only God can do that. They do not have the power to reform their lives and begin to live obediently; only God can do that. They do not have the power to take themselves to heaven; only God can do that.

When Paul wrote in Ephesians 2 that human beings are dead in their sins, that is what he meant; human beings are no more able to save themselves than dead persons are able to resurrect themselves from the dead. Only God can help us.

However, in Ephesians 2 Paul did not say that human beings are unable to respond to the gospel with repentance and faith. We believe that they can respond, that they are responsible to do so, and that they will be held accountable for how they respond. Traditional Baptists believe that human beings are able to repent and have faith in Christ because God created them with that ability.

In that sense repentance and faith are gifts of God. There is a second sense in which repentance and faith are gifts of God, namely, that God has provided in the gospel a message that elicits from human beings a response of repentance and faith. The gospel is the power of God for salvation.[88] Even when we make allowances for the fact that repentance and faith are God's gifts in these two senses, it remains the case that repentance and faith are something that human beings do; they are not gifts of God in the Calvinistic sense that God gives them to the elect human beings apart from any response on their part and does not give them to the reprobate.

The Grace of God

Traditional Baptists believe that God freely offers grace and salvation to all people. The offer is genuine; everyone is able to accept it or reject it. The sovereign God waits upon the decisions of human beings and respects their decisions, saving those who accept the gospel and condemning those who reject it. God's offer of grace and salvation can be rejected and, sadly, it sometimes is.

The sovereign God could have chosen to give grace to an elect group, irresistibly. Traditional Baptists believe that God had the power and the wisdom to do that. But we believe that God sovereignly chose to do something else, namely, to offer grace and salvation as free gifts to all people and to give them to those who accept the offer but not to those who resist it. Grace might have been irresistible, but God sovereignly decided to allow it to be resisted.

This is the traditional Baptist theology as we understand it. As we will see in the following chapter, it matters a great

---

[88]Rom. 1:16.

deal whether we retain the traditional Baptist theology or accept Calvinism.

8

Conclusion

An Important Question

All Calvinism is not alike. In this book we have distinguished Calvinism from hyper-Calvinism, and we have referred in passing to the fact that there are varieties of Calvinism. One of the ways in which Calvinists express the diverse kinds of Calvinism is with reference to the five points of Dort. Some speak of themselves as *five point Calvinists*, others as *four point Calvinists*, and so on. A Calvinist might, for example, have doubts about limited atonement while believing in the other four points in the *Canons of Dort*.

This is quite understandable. There is, however, an important sense in which Calvinism is not a matter of degrees but rather an either/or matter. The either/or question concerns predestination: Did the sovereign God decide in advance to save particular individuals and to damn the others? If we answer that question Yes, we are Calvinists, whatever we may say of the other four points of Dort; if we answer it No, we are not Calvinists, whatever we may say of the other four points.

Traditional Baptists answer that question No. In chapter 7 we attempted to describe the theology to which traditional Baptists say Yes. Now we will attempt to answer the question, What is at stake in this answer? We will do this in two parts. One is to display what we believe to be the most important truth in Christian theology; the other is to describe a very important implication of that truth.

The Most Important Truth

Traditional Baptists believe that the most important truth in Christian theology is this: God is love.[89]

We believe that the love of God lies behind the coming of Jesus Christ and is the reason God sent Christ into the world. "God so loved the world, that He gave His only begotten Son."[90]

Nothing is more important to those of us who are traditional Baptists than this: God so loved the world.

What troubles us most about Calvinism is that Calvinism fails to say clearly and forcefully that God loves the world.

Calvinists believe that, in an important sense, God loves the elect but not the reprobate. As Calvin put it, God "ordained from eternity those whom he wills to embrace in love, and those upon whom he wills to vent his wrath."[91]

---

[89] 1 Jn. 4:8, 16.

[90] Jn. 3:16.

[91] Calvin, *Institutes*, 3.24.17.

Some contemporary Calvinists express this just as forcefully as Calvin did:

> God is the God of distinction. Discriminating distinctions between men are given in the Scriptures, and God is the discriminator. He loves some and hates others. He chooses some and passes by others (Rom. 9:13). He appoints some to salvation and others to wrath (1 Thess. 5:9). God has mercy on some and hardens others (Rom. 9:18). He ordained some to eternal life (Acts 13:48), and He ordained others to condemnation (Jude 4). God knows some and does not know others (John 10:14; Matt. 20:28). God elected some and reprobated others (Eph. 1:4; Rom. 11).[92]

Other Calvinists, however, prefer to express it more mildly. They say that God loves the elect in one way and the reprobate in another, or they say that God loves the elect as the children of God and the reprobate as the children of darkness.

For us the milder expressions are no help at all. We are committed to the position that it is a supremely important Christian teaching that God loves the world. This is the traditional Baptist view. Since love means you act for the welfare of those you love, predestining persons to be damned is not love.

---

[92] W. E. Best, *God Is Love* (Houston: WEBBMT, 1986), 40.

We believe in the love of God for all people because the Bible teaches it and because Jesus displayed it throughout his life and especially at his death.

The love of God for all people is operative throughout the entire Christian religion. For example, it is operative in Christian ethics. It is morally right to treat all people with respect because God loves them all.

The love of God for all people is operative in evangelism and missions. We send missionaries to preach the gospel to all people because God loves all people and wants them all to be saved.

The love of God for all people underwrites the true meaning of our lives. Jesus called us to love the Lord with all our hearts and to love our neighbors as ourselves.[93] The Ten Commandments are guidelines into how to love God and neighbor. Love is the fulfillment of the law.[94] Love is greater than faith or hope.[95] We love because God first loved us.[96]

Nothing is more important to us who are traditional Baptists than this: *God so loved the world, that He gave His only begotten Son, that whoever believes in Him should not perish, but have eternal life.*

Because Calvinism loosens our grip upon the supreme truth of God's love for the world and calls us to think of God as loving some and not others, we reject Calvinism.

---

[93]Mt. 22:34-40.

[94]Rom. 13:10.

[95]1 Cor.13:13.

[96]1 Jn. 4:19.

Unpersuaded by Calvinism's claim to be biblical and unconvinced that is an indispensable part of the Baptist theological
heritage, we respectfully but emphatically decline the invitation of Calvinism. Instead we embrace with all our hearts
the warm-hearted biblical claim, "God so loved the world." In
God's love that is undiscriminating in its warm embrace of all
people lies our hope, our mandate for living, and our motive
for service.

An Important Implication

A very important implication follows from traditional
Baptist theology about God's love.

It concerns two of the most important activities in Baptist
life, evangelism and missions. Most Baptists are committed
to evangelism and missions because they are committed to the
fact that God loves the world and wants the world to be saved.

Traditional Baptists believe that their acceptance or
rejection of Calvinism has implications for their commitments
to evangelism and missions. We believe they are right.

Before we explain why, we want to point out that many
Calvinists have been and are fully committed to evangelism
and missions. The first Baptist missionary to India, William
Carey, was a Calvinist; the evangelistic Baptist pastor in
London at the end of the nineteenth century, Charles Haddon
Spurgeon, was a Calvinist. While hyper-Calvinists have
resisted evangelism and missions, most Baptists today who
are Calvinists are committed to evangelism and missions. We
are very happy that this is the case.

Nevertheless, the way that we respond to Calvinism has implications for our commitment to evangelism, for this reason: The principal motives that drive most evangelistic and missionary work among traditional Baptists are that God loves all people and wants them all to be saved, and that we must share the gospel so people can be saved.

These motives are not available to Calvinists. Since they do not believe that God loves everyone in the sense of wanting everyone to be saved, they do not accept the former motive. And Calvinists cannot conscientiously say things such as, "If we do not preach the gospel to the lost, they can't be saved," because they think that all of the elect will be saved whether or not Christians are faithful to their responsibility to preach the gospel.

Calvinists are aware that they need other motives for evangelism and missions, and naturally they discuss what such motives might be. One example of an alternative motive is this: In the Great Commission (Mt. 28:19-20) Jesus told his followers to go and make disciples, so we must do it. The motive is simply that we must obey his command.

Traditional Baptists share that motive with Calvinists. But, in fact, across the years the motives that have become dominant for us, indeed, almost exclusive for us, are that God loves all people and wants them to be saved and that we must share the gospel so people can be saved. Since these are virtually the only motives at work among us, if we accept Calvinism we risk losing the motives that drive most of our evangelism and missions. If we lose those motives, we could become less evangelistic and less supportive of missions. And that would be a tragedy.

A Final Word

When we introduced this book we said that we hoped to speak the truth in love about Calvinism in order to help traditional Baptists relate to it in a Christian way. Whether we have succeeded or not, our readers will decide. We have done our best.

Our final word is that love is the most important thing of all. Theologically, God's love for all people is most important truth; ethically, God's call to us to love all people is the most important mandate. With that in mind we urge our traditional Baptist readers to respond to Calvinists with love. There is no reason to be angry about Calvinism or frightened by it or to resent it.

One of the most natural assumptions we human beings make is that if we believe something deeply and express it clearly, then anyone who disagrees with us must either be acting willfully or not understanding what we say; in other words, those who disagree with us are either evil or stupid. As we grow older, however, we learn that there are intelligent, honorable people who honestly do not agree with us.

That is the case with Calvinism. Many bright, fine people, including many Baptists in the past, have accepted it. The majority of Baptists today reject it. And that's where the matter stands.

It is possible for traditional Baptists and Calvinists to be friends and to respect and appreciate one another; we know because we have experienced it. We hope that God will give our readers the wisdom they need in order to know how to relate in a Christian way to Calvinism.